Introducing Phonetics

S. S. HAIDER | RAJ KUMAR SHARMA

ATLANTIC
PUBLISHERS & DISTRIBUTORS (P) LTD

ATLANTIC
PUBLISHERS & DISTRIBUTORS (P) LTD
7/22, Ansari Road, Darya Ganj, New Delhi
Tel.: +91-11-4077 5252, 2327 3880
E-mail: orders@atlanticbooks.com
Web: www.atlanticbooks.com

Reprint 2018, 2021, 2023, 2026

Published by Atlantic Publishers & Distributors (P) Ltd.

Printed & bound in India by Atlantic Print Services

Dedicated to

Syed Shamim Haider

and

Sarah Shahnaz Haider

who left us prematurely

Preface

This book deals with the fundamental concepts of phonetics in a very simple and scientific manner. Phonetics is gradually gaining ground in the curriculum of Indian universities keeping in view the growing relevance of oral skills in communication at global level. A shift in the focus of language teaching and learning has already been set in that necessitates primacy of speech over other skills in the technology-driven world. Since phonetics as an area of knowledge helps learners master the nuances of speech, its significance in today's globalized setting can arguably be visualized. With this objective, an effort has been made here to introduce different aspects and components of phonetics that may contribute to the enhancement of oral communication of the learners, especially in the use of the English language. Speaking globally intelligible English continues to be a major challenge for the majority of Indian learners as the degree of interference from their mother tongue in learning English remains very strong. This book takes into account all such challenges encountered by the Indian learners of English and brings out measures to overcome these in a facile and pragmatic manner.

All the ten chapters of the book are scientifically sequenced that facilitate easy assimilation of concepts in a coherent way. Each chapter has a set of exercises that will help the learners in self-evaluation. This book is meant for undergraduate and postgraduate students of English and Linguistics. It may be equally useful to all those who wish to improve their spoken English skills. Many diagrams and charts have been given for adequate illustration of phonetic terms and ideas. Phonetics is a newly emerging branch of knowledge and hence, there is a considerable difference of opinion among phoneticians regarding many of the concepts. An effort has been made here to reason out such concepts but the degree of success in resolving these complex issues will be largely determined by the readers. Therefore, suggestions of the readers that may qualitatively upgrade the contents of the book are always welcome.

S.S. Haider

Raj Kumar Sharma

Acknowledgements

A book is conventionally a product that unfolds the efforts of many people who directly or indirectly contribute to its making. This book, too, is not an exception. It bears the imprint of inspirations and mechanical support of our well-wishers.

We are extremely thankful to Dr. Imtiaz Husnain and Dr. Shagufta Husnain, Senior Faculties of Linguistics at Aligarh Muslim University who went through the manuscript and came out with valuable inputs that made this work rich. Sincere thanks are due to the members of our family who spared us from household responsibilities at the time of intense involvement with this work. We are equally thankful to our colleagues and students with whom we invariably interact over academic issues that largely shape our professional maturity.

We are thankful to Dr. K.R. Gupta, Chairman, Atlantic Publishers & Distributors (P) Ltd., New Delhi, for his earnest efforts without which this book would not have bloomed forth.

S.S. Haider

Raj Kumar Sharma

Contents

1

All about Phonetics and Phonology

The last quarter of the twentieth century witnessed an unprecedented trend of mass inter-cultural and inter-continental migration necessitated primarily by the emerging global market forces that infused a fresh interest among people for learning new languages. The major driving force behind learning a language was to develop linguistic competence, especially speaking skill that really constitutes the biggest portion of all the communicative needs. Further, it was increasingly observed that this growing wave of globalization created a condition for the emergence of a global language. It is relevant to mention here that most of the leading countries that championed the cause of globalization had English as their native language. It largely contributed in catapulting English to the position of global language. Though there are several other factors as well behind the emergence of English as the global language such as historical (language of the potential colonizers), scientific (language of science and technology), socio-cultural (language of upward social mobility), etc., the phenomenal success of globalization as a reality of post-colonial era definitely gave a giant fillip to the status of English that strongly established it as an international language. Today, it would not be an overemphasis to state that globalization and English stand complementary to each other. English undoubtedly has turned out to be the language of globalized world. Learning new languages in general and English in particular in this highly globalized set up has become an inevitable reality. Here comes the role of phonetics that proves to be very handy in mastering speaking skill of the target languages.

1.1 What is Phonetics?

It is a commonly observed fact that language is primarily speech consisted of sound bits and bytes. It is the spoken form of language that is predominantly used by mankind for its variety of communicative needs. This spoken form constitutes almost 85 per cent of the total use of language by an individual in his/her life according to a latest report. This observation holds water simply on the ground that we hardly spend any day on which we do not speak anything, whereas we pass many days without writing in usual conditions. Moreover, writing is only visual representation of speech that is used to preserve what has been spoken at any point of time in present or past with the sole intention of passing it on to the coming generations.

Historically, speech came before writing. A child first listens to and then reproduces only sounds. Even before the first letter of the alphabet has been learnt, a child not only speaks words but also sentences with ease. If we look at the rules of grammar, we will find that they are based on speech rather than writing. Also, nearly 40 per cent of languages exist only in their spoken form.

Keeping in view these facts, any study of language must begin with sounds and not with the visible marks on paper or any other surface. The study of the sounds of language is the central concern of phonetics. According to Abercrombie (1982), "the study of the medium of spoken language, in all its aspects and all its varieties, constitutes the subject of phonetics". He also says that "phonetics is concerned with the medium as used in speaking all human languages (whether 'primitive' or 'civilized') and as used in all styles of speech (whether supposed to be good or bad, normal or abnormal)".

The word phonetics is made of 'phone', which means sound, and 'tics' gives it the status of science. Phonetics is a scientific study of sounds of language in all their aspects. It is a science because in its study of the sounds it employs the methods used by science such as observation, collection of data, analysis and classification of the data collected, and on this basis propound a theory that helps explain the facts of language related to it. Phonetics lays the foundation on which studies on other levels of language can be made. It is responsible for the first level of linguistic analysis (phonological), the other levels being morphological, syntactic and semantic. Phonetics takes into account all kinds of sounds produced by mankind for the purpose of communication. As one of the core branches of linguistics that intends to undertake a scientific study of languages in general, phonetics deals with the number of sounds produced in different languages along with their identification, classification and ways of production.

1.2 Branches of Phonetics

Since language is primarily speech, it implies that someone needs to produce or articulate sounds for others to receive or hear so that some kind of communication takes place. When sounds, linguistic or otherwise, are produced, they travel in the air before reaching the ears of the listener or receiver. How they are transmitted determines the type of communication that takes place. In fact, production or articulation, transmission and reception of sounds are responsible for communication to take place. Therefore, traditionally there are three branches of phonetics but these days much experimentation is underway in phonetics that has resulted into the emergence of a new branch called experimental phonetics. Because of these developments, phonetics may be reasonably divided into four branches: articulatory, acoustic, experimental and auditory.

1.2.1 Articulatory Phonetics

Articulatory Phonetics is concerned with how sounds are produced or articulated, what organs are involved in the production of sounds, and what mechanism results in the production of these sounds, etc. It talks about evolving the parameters for identification and classification of sounds in all the possible ways. It takes into account all the steps involved in production of sounds right from the point of their origin in chest muscles to physical realization outside the oral or nasal cavity.

1.2.2 Acoustic Phonetics

When a speech sound is produced, it moves in the air from the speaker to the listener. The mechanism involved in transmitting speech sounds through air from point of production to the ears of listeners constitutes the subject matter of acoustic phonetics. This transmission of sound is very crucial for the meaning to be understood and purpose of communication to succeed. It determines the physical properties of sounds in relation to the physical environment prevailing outside. The branch of phonetics which studies this aspect of sounds is called Acoustic Phonetics. Sound quality, loudness and amplitude, pitch and intensity, and nasal resonance are some of the features of acoustic make-up of speech. The objective of acoustic phonetics is to study and measure these features. For the purpose of measurement, scientific instruments like pitchmetre, oscillograph, audiometer, etc. are used.

1.2.3 Auditory Phonetics

Once speech sounds reach the ears of the listener, they are carried to the brain by the auditory nerves. The brain then interprets the sound and so communication takes place. If the sounds are not received by the ears, not carried to the brain by the auditory nerves or the brain fails to interpret the sounds, communication breaks down. The ears play a very important role in the communication process. The branch of phonetics responsible for the study of reception of sounds is known as Auditory Phonetics. It is here that sound signals are decoded resulting into the conveyance of the messages or transmission of the ideas.

Hearing is known as the peripheral auditory system. The decoding of sounds which takes place in the neural areas is known as the internal auditory system. The ear is divided into three sections—the outer ear, middle ear and inner ear. The only function performed by the outer ear is to focus the point of entry of the sound waves. When sound travels from the outer to the middle ear, it exerts pressure which sets the bones in vibration and allows the sound waves to be carried into the inner ear. The inner ear located within the skull converts sounds into neural impulses. It is the internal auditory system which breaks down speech into its component parts and thus plays an important role in the communication process.

1.2.4 Experimental Phonetics

Besides the above-mentioned three branches of phonetics, there is another branch which concerns itself with making experiments in order to study the various aspects of speech sounds which can distinguish the same sound in different languages or to bring out the acoustic value of an utterance. This branch of phonetics is called Experimental Phonetics. In order to carry out experiments, instruments are used as in any other science.

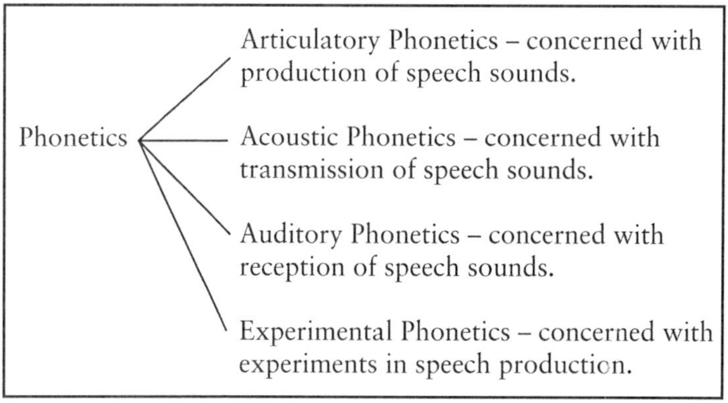

1.3 What is the Relevance of Studying Phonetics?

Phonetics as a branch of knowledge has acquired much significance in modern time. Today's society is marked by rapid expansion of information technology where the role of speech has gained new dimension. The revolution in the field of electronic media has made speech the testing ground of one's communicative ability. Phonetics helps an individual chisel his/her speaking ability as it deals with all the technicalities associated with the correct articulation of different speech sounds. A comprehensive look at the relevance of phonetics leads us to following points.

(a) The findings of phonetics can be effectively used in language teaching, especially in teaching listening and speaking. Incorrect articulation of the sounds of the language being learnt—both in isolation and in connected speech, can result in loss of communication. If the teacher is familiar with the speech mechanism and the ways of articulation of the language being learnt, the problem of incorrect articulation can be overcome. Abercrombie (1982) has observed that "teachers of English have willy-nilly to be phoneticians". In fact, all language teachers have to be phoneticians in order to help the learners with correct pronunciation of the sounds of the language being learnt 'free from dialectal peculiarities' and to 'cure an accent' as Ward (1948) says.

(b) The insights offered by phonetics can be profitably used by curriculum planners and in preparing teaching/learning material, especially in the case of second language teaching/learning. The scientific description of the sounds of the first language and the target language can help contrast the sound systems of the two languages. Error analysis of the learners' speech and contrastive analysis of the learners' first language/mother tongue and the target language/second language can bring out interesting facts and help in preparing teaching/learning material. According to Peter Strevens, "the place of linguistics is in the back room", where curriculum planning and textbook writing takes place. Phonetics, it has to be remembered, is one of the linguistic sciences.

(c) Normal everyday speech is different from elocution, public speech and group discussion. Different strategies have to be adopted to put the ideas across by using different stress patterns, intonation patterns, junctures, etc. Knowledge of phonetics, and its application can be used to train people in charge of admission processes and personal selection.

(d) Phonetics is concerned with the study of articulation of speech sounds. A trained phonetician can easily detect defects of speech and suggest ways for getting over them. Speech therapists can be assisted by trained phoneticians who know how the speech sounds of the language spoken by the patient are articulated.

(e) Insights drawn from phonetics can also help in teaching speech to the deaf by training them how hand movement and lip movement can be coordinated.

(f) Phonetic theory can also be applied to the study of words (philology), and in analyzing and recording various dialects with precision.

(g) In legal trials phoneticians are frequently called as witnesses. They are asked to certify whether the voice on a tape-recorded phone call is likely to be that of the suspect. Experts in acoustic phonetics can offer quantifiable acoustic data to support their opinion.

(h) Tremendous technological development has been taking place in recent times. This has supplemented the resources of the medium by means of various mechanical and electronic devices. Inventions like telephone, radio, recording devices, deaf aids, etc. have raised many problems of communication which are also problems of phonetics. It is in this context that the study of phonetics assumes special importance.

(i) In today's fast growing world, the possibility of inter-cultural migration is umpteen where the learning of new languages is required. Phonetics turns out to be a very handy tool in several ways in developing standard pronunciation skill among such migrants in the best possible way and the shortest possible time. It enables an enthusiastic learner to acquire global intelligibility in the target language very shortly.

(j) In cinema or any dramatic art, the dialogues of the artists can be tested and improved upon very easily with the application of phonetic information in terms of modulation of speech, frequency, amplitude, etc. that certainly exercises profound influence on the quality of these artistic productions.

(k) In the field of cryptography as well that is used by military forces and intelligence services for passing sound signals to different operating groups, the role of phonetic information is very crucial. In coding and decoding of the messages, the technical phonetic inputs become a great facilitator in the entire process.

All these points definitely give phonetics a sound footing in terms of relevance. With passage of time, its popularity is growing very fast as exploratory phonetics is opening many new avenues where phonetic inputs add to the quality of such specific domains.

1.4 Phonology

In our definition of phonetics in Section 1.1, we have seen that it is the scientific study of the sounds of language in all their aspects. It means that it is not concerned with the sounds of any given language. It only gives us a theory on the basis of which we can study the sounds of any language. No two languages use exactly the same sounds and in exactly the same way. It is not the concern of phonetics to study which sounds a particular language uses and in what ways it organizes them. Out of a multitude of available sounds, a language selects only a few and builds its own stock. These sounds are grouped or organized by the language in a way which is usually different from the way another language organizes its sounds. For example, /P/ sound of Hindi is not realized in English exactly in the same way though for a layman it may sound alike. Some sounds may be found in some languages whereas they may be absent in others. For instance, /bh/ and /gh/ are the prominent sounds of Hindi which are not found in English. Likewise, /p/ is not found in Arabic while it appears in many languages of the world. We shall study "The Sounds of English" in Chapter 5. Again, in some African languages, a sound like 'n' can precede the sound 'g' or 'k' in the beginning of a word or a syllable. 'Nkrumah' was the name of a very prominent leader of an African country. But in English this is not possible which shows organizational uniqueness of sound systems operational in a language.

Out of a large number of sounds available, a language selects just a few sounds in order that its speakers can communicate or interact among themselves. This selection of particular sounds in preference to other sounds that are available is not studied by phonetics; it is studied by phonology.

All languages do not organize sounds in the same way as we have seen in the case of English and some African languages. English does not allow a combination of the sounds of '*ps*', '*ts*' or '*ks*' in the beginning of a syllable or a word, but it is possible at the end of a syllable or a word, for example, 'tops', 'hats', 'sticks', etc. The organization of sounds is a unique feature of a language. This again is not studied by phonetics; it is studied by phonology. Abercrombie (1982) writes: "It is this selection from the full general human phonetic range which is formed into the pattern which carries the particular language. The selection and the pattern into which they are formed, constitute the phonology of the language. The phonology of a language is particular to that language and different from that of any other language." A phonological approach also brings out the pattern-forming capabilities of the elements of utterances as used in a particular language, rather than place them in general human phonetic resources. According to Ladefoged (1982), "Phonology is the description of the systems and patterns of sounds that occur in a language. It involves studying a language to determine its distinctive sounds and to establish a set of sounds that describe the set of changes that take place in these sounds when they occur in different relationships with other sounds." For example, the English phoneme /t/ is pronounced in two different ways in words like 'tool' and 'stool'. In the first word it is pronounced as [th] (aspirated), ut in the second word as [t] (unaspirated). These two different sounds are allophones.

Thus, phonology studies the selection and organization of sounds in a language. The operative word is the article 'a'. The difference between phonetics and phonology is that while phonetics is concerned with the study of speech sounds in all their aspects in language as such, phonology restricts itself to the study of selection and organization of sounds in a particular language relying on the findings offered by phonetics. In fact, it has been suggested that the general phonetic approach and the phonological approach to the aural medium complement each other, and both are needed to provide an adequate account of the medium as used for a given language. Both approaches deal with the same facts; they differ in the way the facts are 'selected and grouped in attention.' It is for this reason that Andre Martinet terms phonology as 'functional phonetics.'

Exercise

1. What is phonetics? Discuss the uses of phonetics.
2. What are the branches of phonetics? On what basis has phonetics been divided into these branches?
3. Differentiate phonetics from phonology.

4. Say whether the following statements are true or false.
   (a) Phonetics is the scientific study of the sounds of a language.

   True False

   (b) Auditory phonetics is concerned with the reception of sounds.

   True False

   (c) Phonology studies the selection and organization of sounds in a language.

   True False

   (d) Phonetics and phonology together provide the foundation for the study of other levels of language.

   True False

   (e) Acoustic phonetics studies the articulation of speech sounds.

   True False

   (f) Every language has its own phonology.

   True False

2

Articulation of Speech Sounds

In Chapter 1, we saw that one of the branches of phonetics, Articulatory Phonetics, is concerned with articulation of speech sounds. In this chapter, we shall see how these sounds are articulated. This will include speech mechanism and organs of speech.

2.1 Speech Mechanism

Production of any sound, linguistic or non-linguistic, requires a medium which is air. In fact, sound is said to be modified breathing. Speech is a motor activity which requires energy. This energy is provided by air. The air for the production of speech sounds is provided by the process of breathing or respiration. The air that we breathe in or inhale passes through a channel and reaches the lungs, and, in its journey to the lungs, it passes through different organs located in the channel.

These organs are called organs of speech, though they are primarily used for other purposes. We normally breathe or inhale air through our nose. After entering the nostrils, air goes to the pharynx and then to the larynx from where it travels to the lungs via the trachea. Once the lungs have used this air, they expel it and then it uses the same route to come out of the body. There is one difference, though, and that is this air may also come out through the mouth or the oral cavity. Thus, the speech act involves almost half of human body. It is the result of a well-coordinated or orchestrated action in this part of the body. With the above process in mind, let us proceed to see which organs are involved in modifying the air resulting in speech sounds.

2.2 Organs of Speech

The organs used for speech production fall into three systems—the respiratory system, phonatory system and articulatory system. The respiratory system includes the lungs, bronchial tubes and trachea; the phonatory system consists of the larynx or the voice box; and the articulatory system comprises the nose, lips, and mouth and its contents (the palate, tongue and teeth).

Let us now look at Fig. 2.1 which presents a picture of speech organs. It does not include the bronchial tubes and the lungs, and shows only a part of the trachea.

1-Nasal Cavity
2-Lips
3-Teeth
4-Alveolar/Teeth Ridge
5-Hard Palate
6-Velum (Soft Palate)
7-Uvula
8-Apex (Tip) of Tongue
9-Blade (Front) of Tongue
10-Dorsum (Back) of Tongue
11-Oral Cavity
12-Pharynx
13-Epiglottis

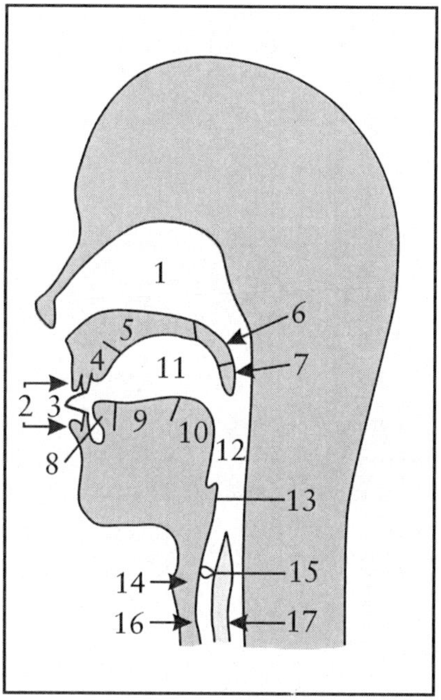

Fig. 2.1: The Organs of Speech

14-Larynx

15-Vocal Cords (Glottis)

16-Trachea (Windpipe)

17-Esophagus (Food Pipe)

Lungs

The air that we breathe in goes to the lungs which use it for purposes other than production of sounds. It is this air which provides energy required for the production of sound. Once this air has been used, it is expelled by the lungs and then finds its way to come out of the body through the oral and/or the nasal cavities.

Bronchial Tubes

Bronchial tubes are small tubes which carry the air to the lungs and take it out of them. They do not participate directly in the production of speech but are important because they carry the air.

Trachea

Trachea or the windpipe is the canal which carries the air to and from the lungs. It is not also directly involved in the production of speech sounds but is important because without it the air cannot reach the lungs.

Larynx

Larynx is located in the upper part of the windpipe and houses the vocal cords or folds. The vocal folds are also known by other names. The vocal cords are responsible for producing sounds, hence larynx is also known as sound box. The larynx is visible in adult males in the shape of a protruded triangular bony structure called Adam's apple.

Glottis

Glottis forms the opening between the vocal cords in the upper part of the trachea. Different types of sounds are produced by the glottis which we shall see when we discuss the sounds of language.

Epiglottis

Epiglottis is a structure of tissues at the root of the tongue, lowered during swallowing of food to prevent it from entering the windpipe.

Pharynx

The pharynx is a cavity at the back of the mouth where the passage to the nose, mouth and larynx begins. This has a role to play in the production of some types of speech sounds.

Uvula

The uvula is a small piece of fleshy matter hanging from the back of the roof of the mouth. It causes obstruction to the passage of outgoing air producing some types of speech sound.

Palate

The palate is located in the oral cavity and forms the roof of the mouth. It is divided into two parts; the hard palate and soft palate. The soft palate is located just at the end of the oral cavity and can be moved. The hard palate stretches from where the soft palate begins to the teeth ridge. It is fixed and cannot be moved.

Teeth ridge

The teeth ridge is located behind the upper row of teeth. It is a slightly raised mass of flesh like a ridge and is also known as alveolar ridge. It represents the beginning of the roof of the mouth.

Tongue

The tongue is a very important organ of speech and is involved in the production of a number of speech sounds. It lies below the palate and is divided into four parts for the purpose of describing speech sounds. They are: (i) the tip or point, (ii) blade, (iii) front and (iv) back. Some phoneticians regard the root of the tongue as the fifth part of the tongue.

Teeth

Of the two rows of teeth, it is the upper teeth that is mostly used for producing speech sounds.

Lips

The lips are also involved in the speech act. Sometimes both lips are used, and sometimes only one is used.

We shall see at length how these organs of speech are used for the production of speech sounds when we discuss the sounds themselves. Note that not all the organs described above are actively involved in the production of speech sounds. Some of these are active articulators, while others are passive articulators. Usually, those located in the lower part of the mouth are active articulators because they can move, and those located in the upper part are passive articulators because they cannot be moved.

The ear, as we have seen in Chapter 1, is responsible for perception and reception of speech sounds produced by the speaker and belongs to the auditory part of speech. Abercrombie (1982), however, suggests that it must be included among the vocal organs. He argues that speech has no value unless it is received as well as it is produced, and the main organ of reception is the ear. According to him, the ear is an important organ to both the speaker and the hearer. This is so because it provides feedback to the speaker of what is being spoken.

The organs used in the speech act are basically the same and also work in the same way in all normal human beings. Everybody who is free from abnormalities of the vocal organs and brain can pronounce any sound.

Exercise

1. Draw a neat diagram of the organs of speech and label it.
2. How do we get the energy required for the articulation of speech sounds?

3. Describe the organs in the articulatory system.
4. What is the role played by the trachea in the production of speech?
5. Say whether the following statements are true or false.
   (a) The phonatory system consists of the uvula and the nasal cavity.

   True False

   (b) When we breathe air goes to the lungs through the trachea.

   True False

   (c) The hard palate is also known as velum.

   True False

   (d) The back of the tongue lies directly under the hard palate.

   True False

   (e) The tip of the tongue and the teeth ridge can together produce many speech sounds.

   True False

   (f) The articulatory system consists of mouth and its contents.

   True False

   (g) Larynx has no role to play in the production of speech sounds.

   True False

   (h) Larynx is visible in adult males in the shape of a protruded structure called Adam's apple.

   True False

6. Fill up the blank spaces with the names of organs of speech.

(a) .... forms the opening between the vocal cords.

(b) .... is located in the upper part of the trachea.

(c) .... is also known as the voice box.

(d) .... is a cavity at the back of the mouth and the larynx.

(e) .... is located in the oral cavity.

(f) .... is a raised mass of flesh like a ridge.

(g) .... is divided into five parts for the purpose of describing speech sounds.

(h) .... are usually located in the lower part of the mouth.

3

Phoneme and Allophone

3.1 Introduction

We saw that every language has its own repertoire or stock of sounds which it uses to communicate meaning. Languages differ from one another in this respect. This is why we cannot understand a language if we are not familiar with the sounds it uses for conveying meaning. The sounds belonging entirely to a language are the phonemes of that language. For example, the sound /p/, as it is produced in words like 'pit', 'spit' or 'apt' in English, belongs to the English language and is a phoneme of this language. This is so because it is not produced in this way in other languages. Language is said to be a system of systems, and one of its systems is the phonological system or the sound system. A phoneme belongs to this system.

Let us look at the following pairs of English words.

pit /sit/	bit /bit/
set /set/	said /sed/
full /ful/	feel /fi:l/

It is very clear that the words in each of the pairs are made of three sounds—*p-i-t* in case of pit, *b-i-t* in case of bit, *s-e-t* in case of set; *s-ai-d* in case of said (the sound produced by 'ai' in said is the same as that produced by 'e' in set); *f-u-ll* in full and *f-ee-l* in feel (*double ee* produces only one sound in the word *feel* and *double ll* in *full* also produces only one sound). These sounds can be said to be the units of these words. If we look at the sounds from this point of view, we can define a phoneme as a unit in the sound system of a language. But this will not be an adequate definition as it will not include all the necessary information about phoneme.

The definition will have to be enlarged. When we analyze the words in pairs above and break them into their sound components, we find that each word is made of three sound units. Any attempt to break the words into more units will prove futile. Each sound is the minimal unit beyond which it cannot be broken. If we include this aspect in our definition, we can say that a phoneme is the minimal unit of sound in the sound system of a language. But this definition will also not bring out all the essential features of the phoneme.

When we look at the above pair of words again, we find that of the three sounds they are made of only one is different. In the first pair, the initial unit/element is different. In the second, it is the last or final unit, and in the third, it is the second or medial unit which is different. This difference of only one unit brings about a difference or contrast in meaning as the meaning of the first word in each pair differs from that of the second because of a difference in only one unit. Such pairs of words, each word of which has a different meaning because of the difference in only one unit, are known as minimal pairs.

Because of this difference in meaning, these units are contrastive in nature. We can now expand our definition further and include the word contrastive in it. We can say that a phoneme is a minimal contrastive unit in the sound system of a language. It is minimal because it cannot be broken into sub-units; it is contrastive because it brings about a contrast or change in meaning; and it is a unit because it is only one of the elements in each of the words.

If we think that our definition of the phoneme is now complete, we are mistaken. Look at the sound 'p' which, we have seen, is a phoneme in English in the words 'pit' and 'spit'. Correct pronunciation of these words will reveal that the sound /p/ is pronounced in two different ways in these words though they belong to the same phoneme. In 'pit' the sound that comes out is '[ph]', while in 'spit' we produce the sound [p]. A phoneme of any language is not pronounced in the same way in all the words in which it occurs; it is articulated differently in different contexts.

These different situations are known as phonetic environment or phonetic context. By this we mean the environment or the context in which a sound occurs, that is, the neighbouring sounds together with their duration, stress and, if voiced, voice pitch. We shall look at terms like stress, voice and voice pitch later. In other phonetic contexts, the letter 'p', representing the phoneme /p/ in English, may be pronounced in different ways and yet they will all belong to the phoneme /p/. F.S. Wingfield defined phoneme as "a group of speech sounds nearly enough alike to be treated as a unit for alphabetic purpose". A phoneme is not an individual sound but a group or bundle of sounds. Jones (1956), who has done pioneering work in the field of phonetics, defines phoneme as "a family of sounds in a given language which are related in character and are used in such a way that no member ever occurs in a word in the same phonetic context as any other member".

Here again a phoneme has not been defined as an individual sound, but as 'a family of sounds' which has many members. These members cannot occur in the same phonetic contexts or situations. We have already seen what phonetic context means. In the words 'pit' and 'spit', the phoneme /p/ occurs in two different phonetic contexts and is articulated in two different ways. In 'pit', it occurs in the initial position in a stressed syllable, that is, it is not preceded by any other sound in the word. Here, it is pronounced as [ph]. But in 'spit', although it occurs in a word or initially in a stressed syllable, it is preceded by another sound and now it is pronounced as [p]. Hence, depending upon the phonetic context, /p/ is pronounced in two different ways in these two words and these two different ways of pronunciation produce two different sounds. It is also important to note that they cannot substitute each other. It is the principal member of the group or family of sounds which is designated as phoneme. The other members are known as allophones.

The phoneme /p/ or any other phoneme is not a physical entity. It is only an abstraction because it is abstracted from a group of sounds and is never realized in the same way in all situations.

We can now say that a phoneme is 'a group of speech sounds' or 'a family of speech sounds' which is a minimal contrastive unit in the sound system of a language. Ladefoged (1982) defines phonemes as "abstract units that form the basis for writing a language systematically and unambiguously".

It is also likely that a phoneme is made of only one member. Such a phoneme is called a monophone.

If we look again at the phoneme /p/ in 'pit' and 'spit', we shall find that this sound is not at all responsible for any meaning by itself. In the word 'pull' or 'poll', it does not give the same meaning as in 'pit' and 'spit'. In various combinations, a phoneme is responsible for various meanings. It is when a phoneme combines with other phonemes, meaning comes out. Thus, a phoneme is not a meaningful unit; it has no intrinsic meaning.

3.2 Identification of Phonemes

In Section 3.1, we saw what a phoneme is. Of the many sounds produced by the speakers of a language, only some can be said to be the phonemes of the language. So how do we say that a particular sound is the phoneme of a language? The phonemes of a language can be established through a procedure called discovery procedure, which is objective and mechanical; does not require intelligence; and if the data is the same, the result will also be the same in all cases. This means that the data constitutes the input which is subjected to discovery procedure, and this yields phonemes which are classified and described.

In Section 1.1, we saw that phonetics is a science since it collects, analyses and classifies the data in an objective manner. Sounds constitute the data of this study. So, all the sounds of the language being studied are collected with the help of a native speaker of the language. This means that all the phones of the sound system have been collected. These are known as raw units because they have not yet been analyzed and classified. This is the phonetic level. Now the phones undergo phonetic transcription, which is narrow transcription. At this stage, the exact sounds, as they have been heard by the native speaker, are represented visually. Having done this, we apply the following four principles:

- Distribution
- Phonetic similarity
- Pattern congruity
- Economy

3.2.1 Distribution

By distribution we mean the environment or context in which a sound or phone occurs. If we can find out all the environments in which a particular sound occurs, we have found the distribution of this sound. This means that we have to find out whether a sound occurs only initially, medially, finally, or in two of these situations, or in all three situations in a syllable; whether it occurs before or after a particular sound and so on. Distribution, according to Swadesh can be of two types—contrastive and complementary.

3.2.1.1 *Contrastive Distribution*: If two sounds can occur in the same phonetic context, they are said to be in contrastive distribution. In our example in 3.1—'pit' and 'bit'—'p' and 'b' occur in the same phonetic context, that is, in the beginning of the word or syllable; they can also occur in other positions as in the words 'cap' and 'cab' and can be replaced by each other. This, however, will result in a change of meaning. So, if some sounds/phones can occur in the same phonetic context and can replace each other and this replacement leads to a change in meaning, they are in contrastive distribution and are designated as phonemes of the language under study. We then apply phonemic transcription or broad transcription to represent the phoneme visually. Conventionally, phonemes are written within slant lines, so 'p' will be written as /p/ and 'b' as /b/.

3.2.1.2 *Complementary Distribution*: If two sounds cannot occur in the same phonetic context or cannot replace each other leading to a change in meaning, they are said to be in complementary distribution. In our example from English in 3.1, that is, 'pit' and 'spit', the letter 'p' represents two different sounds. In 'pit' it represents the sound [ph], while in the word 'spit' it represents the sound /p/. In 'pit', '[p^h]' occurs initially in a monosyllabic stressed word but [p] does not occur initially although the word may be stressed. So we find that these two sounds do not occur in the same phonetic context. But if we pronounce the 'p^h' of 'pit' as 'p' and the 'p' of 'spit' as 'p^h', the meaning of the two words will still remain the same as opposed to our example of /p/ and /b/. 'p' and 'p^h' are, therefore, in complementary distribution.

The sounds which are in complementary distribution are the allophones, a term coined by B.L. Whorf of a phoneme. A group of segments/units in complementary distribution constitute a phoneme. It must be remembered that allophones are not grouped into phonemes by nature but by the phonology of a particular language. They are the contextually determined variants of a phoneme. The sound designated as phoneme is the principal member, and the sounds which are designated as allophones are the sounds which are the subsidiary members of the group or family of sounds. Allophones are represented by using narrow transcription. This is also known as allophonic transcription. For allophonic or narrow transcription, we use square brackets. So [p] and [p^h] in the sound system of English will be shown as [p] and [p^h]. [p] and [p^h] are allophones in English.

In conclusion, we can say that, if two sounds occur in a language in the same phonetic context, that is, where one occurs the other can also occur, they are phonemes of the language. If two sounds cannot occur in the same phonetic context, that is, where one occurs the other cannot occur, they are allophones of the same phoneme.

3.2.2 Phonetic Similarity

In order to be designated as phoneme of a language, the sounds must satisfy another criterion. This is known as phonetic similarity. In English, [p] and [ph] belong to the same phoneme, that is, [p] and [ph] are, therefore, allophones of this phoneme. Their phonetic features are similar because both are voiceless, bilabial and plosives. They belong to the same phoneme. On the other, /p/ as in 'spit' and /b/ as in 'bit' are two different phonemes in English because although both /p/ and /b/ are bilabial plosives, the former, as we have seen above, is voiceless while the latter is voiced. Thus, they share some phonetic features but not all and so lack phonetic similarity. Phonetic features are not language specific.

3.2.3 Pattern Congruity

While allophones [p] and [ph] belong to the same phoneme, /p/ and /b/ are two different phonemes in English because of yet another factor. The pattern in English is that if two sounds are produced by the same organs of speech and their manner of articulation is also the same but one is voiced and the other is voiceless, they will be in contrastive distribution, and shall be treated as separate phonemes responsible for a change in meaning. We have seen that both /p/ and /b/ are bilabial and plosive, but the former is voiceless and the latter is voiced. In English they are two different phonemes. In some other language, however, they may not be two different phonemes but allophones of the same phoneme if this pattern does not exist in that language.

3.2.4 Economy

By economy we mean that if two analyses yield different numbers of phonemes, then the one which yields fewer number of phonemes will be preferred because it will be easier and quicker to learn and will be cost-efficient in typewriting, printing and even writing. English has forty-four phonemes but, if according to some other analysis, the number comes to fifty, it will not be accepted unless some new facts about the language come to light.

3.3 Distinctive Feature Theory

This is a theory that deals with analysis and identification of phonemes in terms of some distinctive features. In Section 3.1, we have looked at the concept of phoneme from the structural point of view, which considers it to be the smallest unit in the sound system of a language. We also saw how a phoneme has different features. For example, the phoneme /p/ is voiceless, bilabial, plosive and can be aspirated or unaspirated, lip-rounded or lip-spread and so on. Another school of linguistics however, did not consider the phoneme as the smallest unit but looked at some distinctive features. According to R. Jakobson of the Prague School, each segment is a 'simultaneous bundle of specified features'. A segment is considered to consist of a number of features called 'matrix', which defines the specific property of a particular segment. These features were stated in terms of acoustic characteristics. However, in 1968 Chomsky and Halle modified the model and redefined the distinctive features in terms of articulatory characteristics. These features are represented in binary terms, that is, '+' and '–', where '+' indicates that a particular sound has got this feature and '–' indicates the absence of this feature. As for instance, /p/ is + bilabial, + plosive and – alveolar, – fricative, etc. In this way, sounds are characterized in terms of their distinctive features as per this theory.

Exercise

1. The phoneme is the minimal contrastive unit in the sound system of a language. Elaborate and exemplify.
2. What do you understand by 'phonetic environment'? Answer with examples.
3. Why does Daniel Jones define a phoneme as a 'family of sounds'? Give examples in support of your answer.
4. Discuss the procedure for discovering the phonemes of a language.
5. Distinguish with examples the difference between contrastive and complementary distribution.
6. What do you understand by the term 'allophone'? Can they be predicted?
7. Discuss the distinctive features theory as expounded by Chomsky and Halle.
8. Write a note on phonetic transcription.
9. Say whether the following statements are true or false.
   (a) A phoneme is a family of sounds.
   True False
   (b) Sounds in contrastive distribution are called allophones.
   True False
   (c) The principal member of a group of sounds is the allophone.
   True False
   (d) Phonemes and allophones are language-specific.
   True False
   (e) A diphthong consists of two vowels within a syllable.
   True False
   (f) A phoneme is a meaningful unit of sound.
   True False

(g) There are two types of distribution.

True False

(h) Two sounds occurring in the same phonetic context.

True False

(i) Conventionally, phonemes are written within slant lines.

True False

(j) Broad transcription is used for representing allophones.

True False

4

The Speech Sounds

Human sounds used in different languages exhibit certain characteristics that determine the classification of these sounds into two broad categories of vowels and consonants. It must also be remembered that these two categories are universal and not language-specific like phonemes. Vowels and consonants are different from each other in form as well as function. They are the segments which constitute a syllable. In this chapter we shall try to understand how these two types/classes of speech sounds are articulated and how they are different from each other.

4.1 Vowels

In Chapter 2, we saw how sounds are articulated and what organs of speech are involved in this act. The organs involved in the articulation of vowels are the tongue, the palate, the glottis and the lips. Going back to the examples in 3.1, that is, pin-bin, set-said, full-feel, we find that all these words are constituted of three units or phonemes. For the first and the last sounds, the air encounters some kind of obstruction while going out. But when we produce the medial sounds, that is /i/, /e/, /u/ and /i:/, the outgoing air does not encounter any obstruction of any type at any point. We also find that the air escapes freely through the mouth and the central tract.

We have seen earlier that glottis is one of the organs of speech. Glottis can be in four different states—(i) wide apart,

(ii) loosely held together, (iii) completely shut and (iv) narrow. If the glottis is wide apart the sound produced will have no vibration, if it is held loosely together the sound produced will have vibration, if it is completely shut the sound produced will not be a vowel but a consonant because the outgoing air will not have a free passage and the sound that is produced in the fourth state of the glottis is whisper. The sounds which do not have vibration are called voiceless sounds and the sounds which have vibration are called voiced sounds.

When the outgoing air passes through the larynx, the glottis or vocal folds vibrate; they are loosely held together. So these sounds are voiced. This is quite different from the way the initial and the final sounds in the above examples are produced. These medial sounds are classified as vowels. So we can say that "a vowel is a voiced sound during the production of which air escapes freely through the mouth, there being no obstruction or narrowing that may cause audible friction."

In the production of these sounds two organs of speech never come in contact or are close enough to produce friction. When these sounds are produced, the air freely goes out of the mouth. The only thing that happens is that some part of the tongue moves but again not so much as to come in contact with any other organ of speech and the lips assume a particular shape. When the tongue moves, it assumes a convex shape or in the words of Peter Ladefoged it is 'domed upwards'.

Let us now see how these vowels are determined and classified in a language. This is done with the help of the cardinal vowel scale.

4.2 Cardinal Vowel Scale

We have seen in 2.1 that the tongue, one of the organs of speech, is divided into the tip, the blade, the front, the back and the root. Now let us produce the sound 'i:' as in 'peel' and 'u:' as in 'pool'. We find that for the former it is the front and for the latter it is the back of the tongue which is used. Let us now take the following pair of words—bar and bee. For the production of 'a:' in 'bar' the tongue is at a very great distance from the soft palate but when we produce 'i:' sound of 'bee' the front of the tongue goes up towards the hard palate and comes very close to it but does not touch it. If we take it further up there is a possibility of its touching the palate. If it happens there will be an obstruction to the passage of air and the result will be that a vowel sound will not be produced because for the production of a vowel sound, we have seen, there should be no obstruction or narrowing of the vocal tract.

We have seen that for the production of vowels we can take (i) the front of the tongue to a very high point but without touching the palate, (ii) the back of the tongue to a very high point but without touching the palate, (iii) keep the front of the tongue very far from the palate and (iv) keep the back of the tongue very far from the palate. Corresponding to this we will have a front area, a back area, a high area and a low area. The following diagram will make it clear.

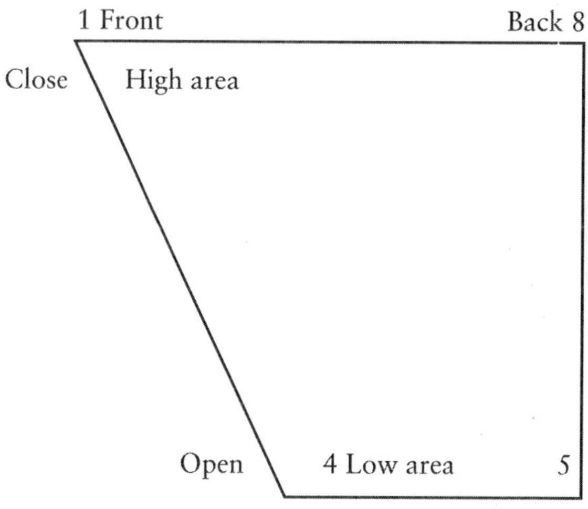

Here, 1 is the highest point to which the front of the tongue and 8 is the highest point to which the back of the tongue can be raised. Similarly, 4 and 5 are the lowest points at which, respectively, the front and the back of the tongue can lie. This area is called the vowel area and the boundary is known as periphery. Any sound produced outside this area will not be a vowel. If the front of the tongue is used for producing a vowel sound, the vowel is a front vowel and if the back of the tongue is used for producing the vowel, it will be a back vowel. So 1 and 4 are front vowels and 5 and 8 are back vowels. Again, if for the production of a vowel sound the tongue is raised to the highest possible point, that is high area, the vowel produced will be a close vowel and if the tongue is at the greatest distance from the palate, that is, in the low area the vowel produced will be an open vowel. Thus 1 and 8 are close vowels and 4 and 5 are open vowels. We can combine the two criteria and call 1 a front close vowel, 4 a front open vowel, 5 a back open vowel and 8 a back close vowel.

Between 1, 8 and 4, 5 we can draw two equidistant parallel lines. The points connecting below 1 and 8 can be 2 and 7 and the lines connecting below 2 and 7 will be 3 and 6. 2 is below the front close vowel. It is called half close front vowel. 7 which is below the back close vowel is back half close vowel. Point 3 is above 4 and is called front half open vowel and point 6 which is above point 5 is the back half open vowel. The following figure will make it clear.

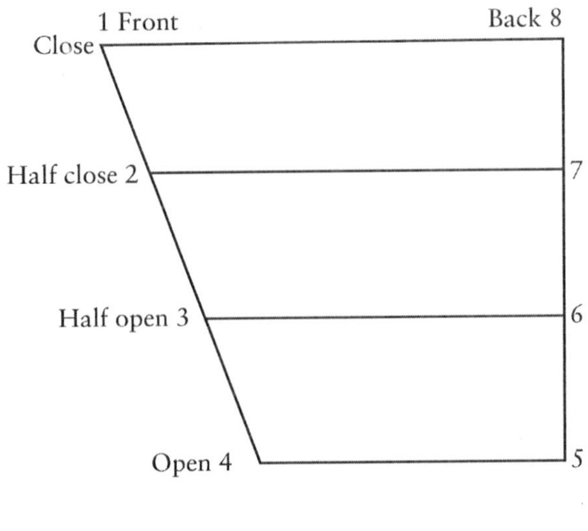

For the production of vowels we can designate an area between the front and the back as the centre. Vowels are also produced from this area. Such vowels are called central vowels. This is shown in the following diagram.

The above description makes it clear that a very large area in the mouth is used for the articulation of vowels making it difficult to describe them. Attempts were made to resolve the difficulty and in 1844, A.J. Ellis put forth the idea of cardinal vowel system. Later A.M. Bell used the word cardinal in 1867. In 1877, Henry Sweet adopted the idea while discussing vowels. However, it was much later that Daniel Jones developed this idea and it is this which is now in use. The system is called cardinal vowel system in a general phonetic sense.

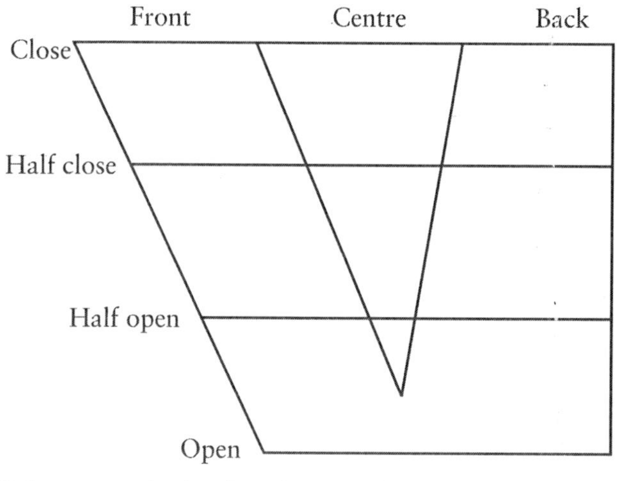

We have seen in 4.1 that there is a limit to which the tongue movement can take place. Keeping in view this constraint Jones devised the cardinal vowel scale. He did so in three stages. In the first stage he set up two points: (i) the highest and front-most point which he designated cardinal vowel number 1 and (ii) the lowest and back-most point which he designated cardinal vowel number 5. In the second stage he fixed three equidistant points pronounced with unrounded shape of the lips in the front periphery and called them cardinal vowels 2, 3 and 4. In the third and final stage he added three more points between cardinal vowel 1 and cardinal vowel 5 on the back periphery and named them cardinal vowels 6, 7 and 8. These three cardinal vowels are articulated with the rounded shape of the lips. Later Jones added eight more cardinal vowels at the earlier points with the difference that the unrounded ones became rounded and the rounded ones became unrounded. Finally, two cardinal vowels in the central region constituted cardinal vowels 17 and 18, the first being unrounded and the second rounded. Cardinal vowel numbers 1 to 8 are called primary cardinal vowels, cardinal vowel numbers 9 to 16 are called secondary cardinal vowels and cardinal vowel numbers 17 and 18 are called tertiary cardinal vowels. It should be noted that all of these occur on the periphery of the vowel area.

Jones did not assign any other articulatory point for cardinal vowels. However, some articulatory points have been added by the International Phonetic Association in the non-peripheral areas as well. The following figure will make it clear.

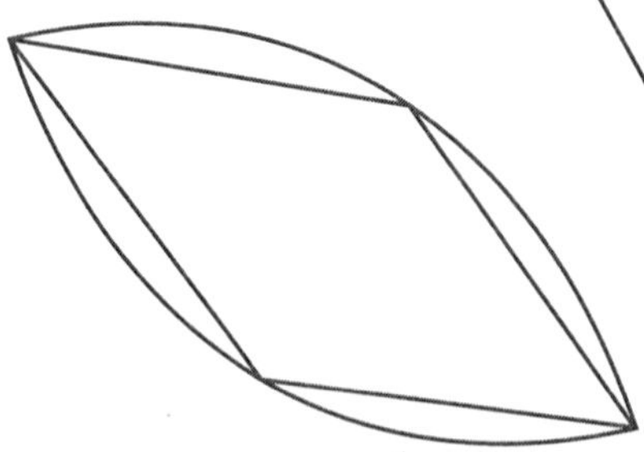

1

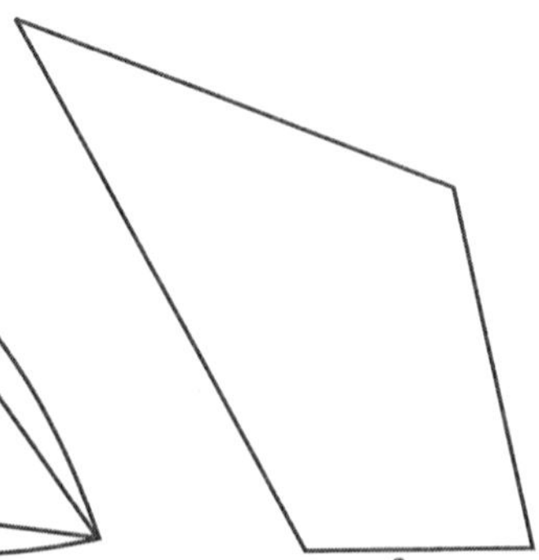

2

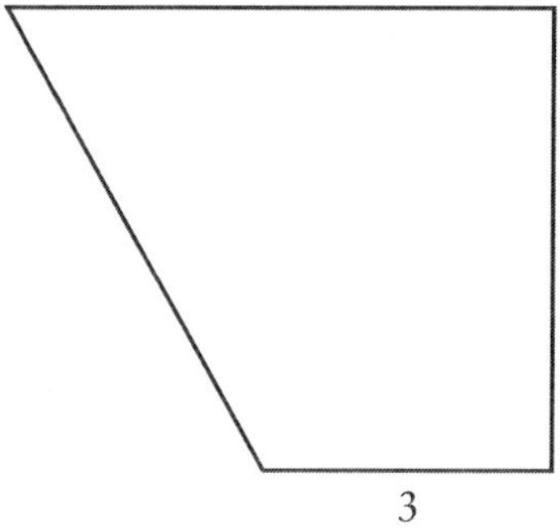

Three stages of finalizing cardinal vowel figure

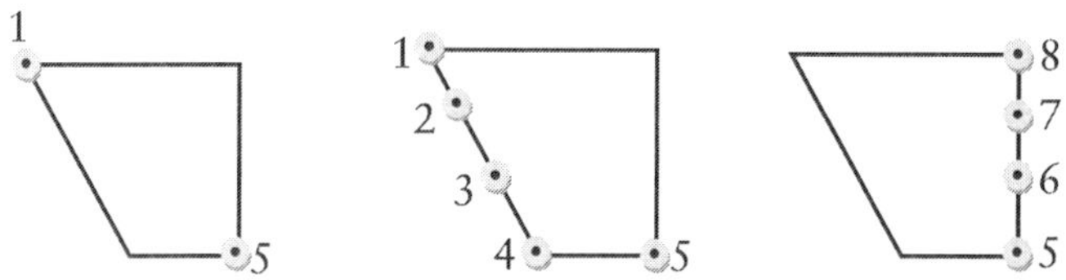

Three stages of fixing cardinal vowels

It is the cardinal vowel scale devised by Jones which is still used for the classification and description of the vowel system in a language, though objections to the system were raised in respect of the difficulty in learning it.

Now let us go back to our example in 4.2 that is 'peel' and 'pool'. If we look into a mirror while speaking these words we shall find that when we produce the 'i:' sound of 'peel' the lips are in a spread or unrounded shape while for the production of 'u:' as in 'pool' they are rounded. This, that is shape of the lips, is an important criterion for classifying and describing the vowels. If the lips are spread the resultant vowel will be lip spread or unrounded and if the lips are rounded the resultant vowel will be lip rounded. There can be different degrees of lip rounding.

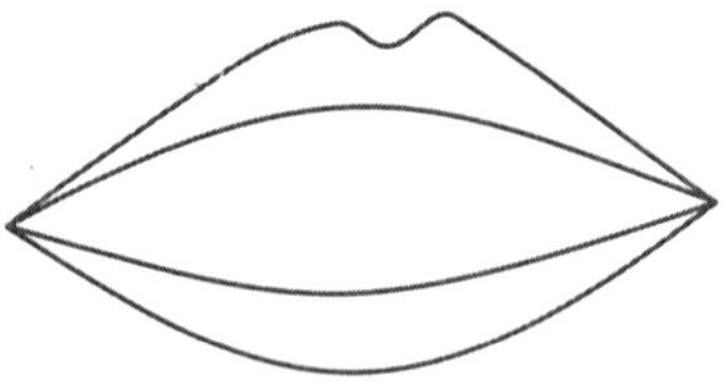

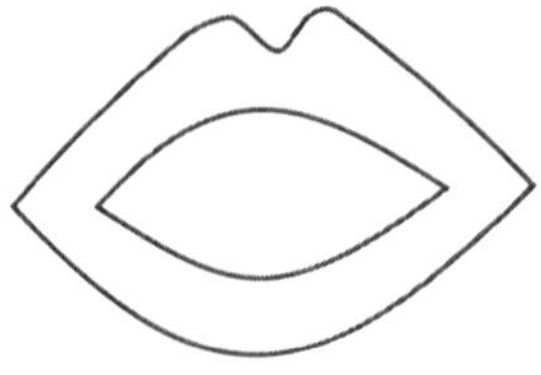

Lip spread/Unrounded **Lip rounded**

The vowels described above are called cardinal vowels and the different points and ways of articulation refer to cardinal vowel scale. These cardinal vowels are imaginary vowels fixed in an arbitrary manner which may or may not actually be found in a language. They are 'language neutral', are exactly determined and their quality is invariable. It should also be noted that they are all peripheral and auditorily equidistant. The cardinal vowel scale is used as a reference point for classifying and describing the vowels of a language. We shall see this when we describe the vowels of English in 5.1.

Thus, in order to describe a vowel, we have to consider the following factors:

(i) part of the tongue raised
(ii) height upto which the tongue is raised
(iii) shape of the lips.

The first yields front, central and back vowels, the second gives close, half close, half open and open vowels and the third rounded and unrounded vowels. This gives us the three-term labels for vowels. As we have already seen all the vowels are voiced. So we do not consider the state of the glottis when we classify and describe vowels.

There is one more aspect of the vowel sound which we need to consider. When we put our fingers below the chin we find that in the articulation of some vowels there is some stiffness at this place while this is not present when we produce other vowels. When we produce the vowels 'i:' and 'u:' in 'peel' and 'pool', respectively, we feel this stiffness or tenseness. Such vowels are called tense vowels. The vowels in the production of which this stiffness or tenseness is not found are called lax vowels. All close vowels are tense.

All these vowels are made of only one sound and are called pure vowels or monophthongs.

4.3 Diphthong

In some cases, however, in the production of a vowel sound the tongue moves from the point of one vowel towards that of another. In such a case the vowel consists of two sounds but they are regarded as one. For example, in the production of the vowel in the word 'now', the tongue first goes up to the point for the production of 'aa' and then moves towards the point for the production of the vowel 'u'. This means that the quality of such a vowel segment is not constant but changes during the course of its articulation. This can clearly be observed by both the ear and the eye. Thus in order to describe a diphthong we have to consider the beginning and the ending points and both vowels have to be described in full. However, the movement from one sound to the other is on the shortest path. It has to be remembered that the tongue does not actually reach the point from where the second vowel is produced. A vowel like this which consists of two different vowel sounds is known as vowel glide or diphthong.

In identifying a sequence of two vowel segments as a diphthong we must ascertain that it belongs to a single syllable. If a sequence of two vowel segments does not belong to the same syllable it will not be a diphthong and has to be treated as two different vowels. Thus the sequence in 'being' belongs to two different syllables and therefore cannot be treated as a diphthong but the sequence in 'fate' /feit/ belongs to the same syllable and therefore it is a diphthong.

4.3.1 Types of Diphthong

Diphthong can be classified on the basis of (a) duration and intensity and (b) direction of tongue movement.

(a) If the first element of a diphthong is of greater duration and intensity it will be a falling diphthong and if the second element is of greater duration and intensity it will be a rising diphthong.

(b) When we look at tongue movement in the articulation of a diphthong we find that it takes place in three directions—from opener towards closer, from closer towards opener and towards the central part. If the tongue moves from an opener towards a closer position it will be a closing diphthong, if the tongue movement is from a closer towards an opener position it will be an opening diphthong and if the movement of the tongue is towards the central part it will be a centring diphthong.

4.3.2 Triphthong

In some cases a vowel may be constituted of three instead of one or two elements. In a situation like this the tongue glides from an initial position to a medial position and then it changes direction to a third position. In order to be designated a triphthong the sequence must belong to a single syllable as it happens in the case of a diphthong. For example, in a word like 'hour' three vowels /a:/, /U/ and /ə/ occur in the same syllable representing a triphthong.

4.4 Vowel Length

We have seen that a vowel can either be long or short. For example, /i:/ is a long vowel but /i/ is a short vowel. These two vowels are different from each other. However, the length of the same vowel may vary according to its phonetic environment. If we pronounce the words 'feast', 'feat', feed' and 'fee' we shall find that although the vowel in these words is the same, its length varies. The vowel in 'fee' is longer than the vowel in 'feed' and the vowel in 'feed' is longer than the vowel in 'feat'. In the same way the vowel in 'feat' is longer than the vowel in 'feast'. This is because of the phonetic environment. In 'fee' the vowel occurs finally and is followed by silence. In 'feed' it is followed by a voiced sound, in 'feat' by a voiceless sound and in 'feast' there are two consonants after the vowel. Thus if a vowel occurs finally its duration will be longer than the duration of the same vowel if it is followed by another sound, a consonant, and if this consonant is voiced the vowel in this word will be longer than the same vowel if the following consonant sound is voiceless and if the vowel is followed by two consonant sounds its duration or length will be shorter than the length of the same vowel if it is followed by a single consonant. Vowel length is also known as quantity. The vowel length is allophonic in nature because it can be predicted.

4.5 Vowel Quality

The quality of a vowel is determined by the shape of the vocal tract. We have to take into account the shape of the lips which can be unrounded and rounded with different degrees of lip rounding, height of the tongue, part of the tongue raised and the part of the palate towards which it is raised. If we look at cardinal vowels /i/ and /u/ we shall find that for the former the lips are unrounded, the front of the tongue is raised and it is raised towards the hard palate but for the articulation of the latter the lips are rounded, it is the back of the tongue which is raised but although it is raised to the same height as for /i/, it is not raised towards the hard palate but towards the soft palate. So the quality of these two vowels is different. According to David Abercrombie, "the distinctive quality of sound of any vowel segment results from the general shape given to the mouth and throat during its production. The mouth and throat together form a tube-shaped cavity which starts at the larynx and ends at the lips and the configuration of this tube, which we call the vocal tract, is moulded by the action of the articulators: it depends partly on the position which the tongue takes up in the mouth and throat, and partly on how the lips shape the exit from the cavity." Apart from the above three factors that is, the height of the tongue, part of the tongue used and shape of the lips, nasalization and retroflexion also determine the vowel quality. It should be remembered that in some languages vowels are nasalized and in some there is curling of the tongue tip for the articulation of vowels. This is also known as rhotacization. The vowel quality can also play a role in the study of the sound system of a language.

4.6 Consonants

We have seen in 4.1 that a voiced sound in the production of which there is no obstruction or narrowing in the vocal tract to cause audible friction is a vowel. All other sounds which are not produced in this manner are consonants. So consonants are those speech sounds which may or may not be voiced and in the production of which there is either obstruction or narrowing at some point in the vocal tract. As a result of this the air cannot escape continuously and freely. In our example in 3.1—'pin' and 'bin', 'set' and 'said' and 'full' and 'feel'—the first and the last sounds in each of these words cannot be articulated unless there is some kind of obstruction or narrowing in the vocal tract. But the medial sounds in these words cannot be articulated if there is any obstruction or narrowing; they can be produced only if the air is allowed to escape freely and there is no obstruction or narrowing. These sounds, therefore, are vowels. Consonants, we should note, occur either in the beginning or end of the syllable. They constitute the marginal elements in a syllable.

4.7 Difference between Vowel and Consonant

We have seen that vowels and consonants are different in terms of articulation. This means that they are different in form. They are also different in yet another respect. The vowels function as the central element in a syllable as in our examples above but consonants do not occur in this position; they are always marginal elements. (We shall see what a syllable is in Chapter 6 but for now it will be defined as part of a word which can be spoken with one puff of air and contains a vowel and may or may not contain a consonant. It can also be a word, for example, 'I'.) So vowels and consonants also differ in function. Thus the difference between vowels and consonants is both phonetic and phonological, that is, how they are articulated and how they function in a syllable. According to Abercrombie, "the stream of air expelled by the chest-pulse can be both released and arrested by accessory articulatory movements. These movements produce the consonants of the syllable. A consonant is a segment of a syllable. Strictly speaking, it is a point in the constantly changing stream of speech, but we treat this point, for purposes of description, as if it were frozen in time."

4.8 Classification and Description of Consonants

We shall now see how consonants are classified and described. In 4.4, we saw that a sound produced as a result of obstruction or narrowing of the vocal tract is a consonant. In 2.5 and 2.6, we saw that the obstruction or narrowing can take place at different points and can be of different types. Depending on this we have different types of consonants. The consonants also differ from one another depending on the state of the glottis. In some languages such as Hindi and Urdu presence or absence of aspiration is yet another factor taken into account for the purpose of classification and description of consonants. Yet another factor is the position of the soft palate. We have to see whether it is raised, lowered or partly raised. The air used for the articulation of the sound has also to be considered. Thus the following factors are considered for classification and description of consonants:

(i) air-stream mechanism
(ii) position of the soft palate
(iii) state of the glottis
(iv) place of articulation
(v) manner of articulation
(vi) aspiration in some languages such as Hindi and Urdu.

Let us now look at these factors in detail.

4.8.1 Air-stream Mechanism

(i) Air-stream mechanism can be of the following types.

(a) Pulmonic

(b) Glottalic

(c) Velaric

(d) A combination of the above

(a) *The Pulmonic Air-stream Mechanism*: We have seen in Chapter 2 that the lungs constitute one of the organs of speech. The air that goes to the lungs is used for the articulation of sounds. This air-stream is known as the pulmonic air-stream. For this air-stream it is the walls of the lungs which act as the initiator. This air-stream is the basis of almost all human speech.

(b) *Glottalic Air-stream Mechanism*: In some cases it is the air which is found in the glottis that is used for the production of speech. This air-stream is known as the glottalic air-stream. The glottis constitutes the initiator for this air-stream. It is also known as the pharyngeal air-stream, particularly in America. Languages of Caucasus, Africa, and central and North America use this air-stream. Because the volume of air controlled by this air-stream is not sufficiently large, it is not found suitable as a mechanism for continuous talking.

(c) *Velaric Air-stream Mechanism*: For this air-stream it is the air above the velum which is used for the articulation of speech sounds. The velum, therefore, acts as the initiator. It is also known as oral air-stream in America.

The process of breathing involves two stages namely inhalation and exhalation. In the first the air goes in and this gives us ingressive air-stream and in the second the air goes out and this gives us egressive air- stream. Thus the air-streams may be pulmonic ingressive and pulmonic egressive, glottalic ingressive and glottalic egressive and velaric ingressive and velaric egressive. Velaric egressive air-stream is not reported to have been used anywhere for the production of speech sounds. English uses primarily the egressive air-stream mechanism for the articulation of all its sounds. However, the first segment of 'yes' when spoken in a somewhat off hand manner uses pulmonic ingressive air-stream mechanism.

(d) *Combined Air-stream Mechanism*: In some cases two air-streams are combined in order to produce a segment of speech. For example, velaric egressive and pulmonic ingressive air-streams or pulmonic egressive and velaric egressive air-streams are combined to produce speech segments in some languages.

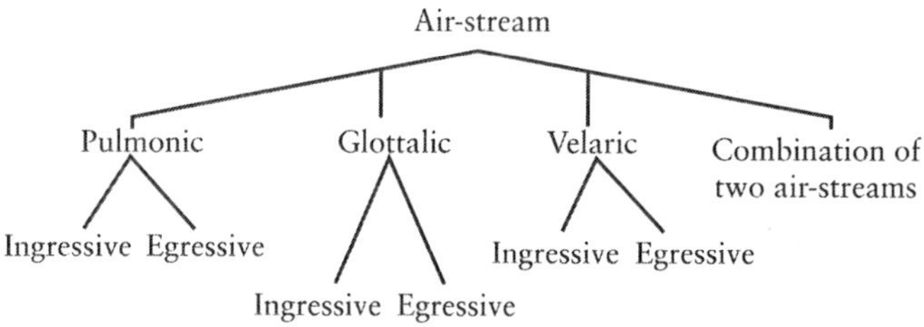

4.8.2 Position of the Soft Palate

We have seen that the soft palate is flexible and can assume different positions.

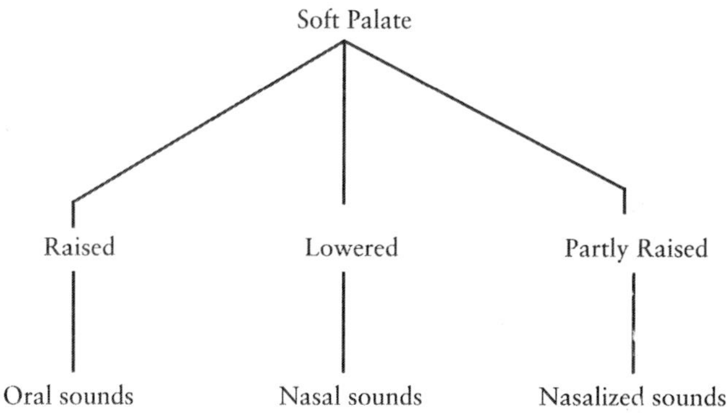

The soft palate can be in a raised position. In this position it does not allow the air to pass through the nasal cavity. Sounds produced in this position of the soft palate are oral sounds such as the sounds in words like 'soft', 'palate', etc.

It can be in a lowered position. In this position it does not allow the air to pass through the oral cavity and the resultant sounds are nasal sounds such as the first and last sounds of the word 'man'. In the third position, it is partly raised and allows the air to pass through the nasal cavity as well as the oral cavity producing nasalized sounds such as the last sound of the Hindi/Urdu word 'haan' (yes).

4.8.3 State of the Glottis

The glottis can be found to be in four states.

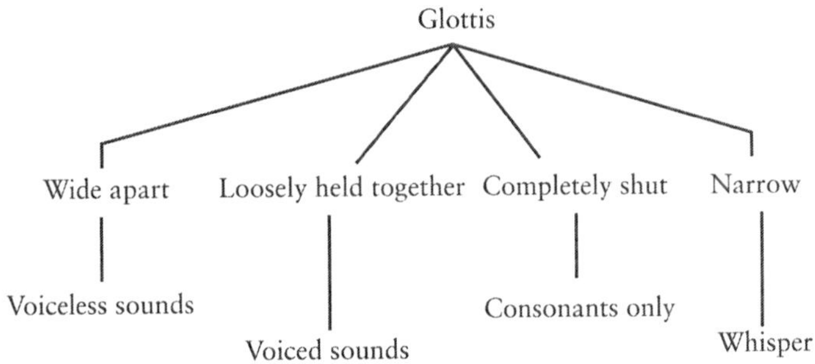

(a) If the glottis, an opening between the vocal folds, is wide apart the sounds produced will have no vibration. Sounds produced without vibration are known as voiceless sounds. (b) If, on the other hand, it is loosely held together there will be vibration. Sounds produced in this state of the glottis are called voiced sounds. Unlike vowels, consonants can either be voiceless or voiced. (c) The glottis can be completely shut producing a sound which can neither be called voiced nor voiceless. (d) Glottis can also be narrow and the sound produced will be whisper.

4.8.4 Place of Articulation

We have seen that speech sounds are produced when the outgoing air encounters some kind of obstruction in the vocal tract. We shall now see which organs are responsible for producing the various types of obstructions. Generally two organs of speech or articulators are involved in the production of speech sounds, particularly for the consonants. Of the two only one moves. The one located in the lower part of the mouth moves to/towards the one located in the upper part. The former is called active articulator and the latter is called passive articulator. Thus when the sound 'd' is articulated, the tip of the tongue is the active articulator and the teeth ridge or the alveolar ridge is the passive articulator. Let us now see which organs of speech are responsible for the obstruction and what the resultant sounds are. Sounds are generally named after the passive articulator.

4.8.4.1 Both lips, the lower and the upper lip, can form obstruction to the passage of air. The lower lip either comes in contact with the upper lip or moves close to it. Sounds produced by both lips are called bilabial sounds.

4.8.4.2 In another situation the lower lip and the upper row of teeth act as active and passive articulators, respectively. Sounds produced by these organs are called labio-dental sounds.

4.8.4.3 The tip of the tongue and the back surface of the upper row of teeth or the opening between the two rows of teeth can form the obstruction. The resultant sounds are called dental sounds. They are also called inter-dental sounds.

4.8.4.4 The tip of the tongue can act as the active articulator while the teeth ridge or the alveolar ridge acts as the passive articulator. This results in the production of alveolar sounds. Such sounds are also known as apico-alveolar sounds.

4.8.4.5 Sometimes the tip of the tongue may move to a point a little behind the alveolar ridge towards the hard palate producing sounds known as post-alveolar sounds.

4.8.4.6 The tip of the tongue is curled and brought in contact with the hard palate. In such a case retroflex sounds are produced.

4.8.4.7 The tip and blade of the tongue and the teeth ridge and the front of the tongue and the hard palate combine to cause obstruction to the passage of the air and produce sounds known as palato-alveolar sounds.

4.8.4.8 The front of the tongue and the hard palate also act together as articulators and produce sounds known as palatal sounds.

4.8.4.9 As we move down the oral cavity or the mouth we reach the back of the tongue. Above this lies the soft palate also known as the velum. When the back of the tongue and the velum act as active and passive articulators, respectively, the resultant sounds are velar sounds.

4.8.4.10 Just after the soft palate lies the uvula. The outgoing air can also encounter obstruction at this point. When the back of the tongue is raised to and retracted from the uvula, the sound produced is called uvular.

4.8.4.11 The pharynx located below the uvula also creates obstruction to the outgoing air producing sounds known as pharyngeal sounds. In this case the back and root of the tongue are retracted into the upper pharynx.

4.8.4.12 One of the states of the glottis is the completely shut state. The sounds that are produced in this state of the glottis are known as glottal sounds.

4.8.4.13 Sometimes, besides the main articulators there is also a co-articulator. For example, the lips can be the main articulators and the hard palate can function as the co-articulator. A sound produced by these articulators is called labio-palatal.

4.8.4.14 Similarly the lips can be the main articulators and the soft palate can function as the co-articulator. Sounds produced by these articulators are called labio-velar sounds.

The following chart will prove helpful in understanding and remembering the place of articulation of the consonant sounds.

Active articulator	Passive articulator	Co-articulator	Sound produced
Lower lip	Upper lip		Bilabial
Lower lip	Upper row of teeth		Labio-dental
Tip of the tongue	Back surface of the upper Row of teeth		Dental
Tip of the tongue	Teeth ridge		Alveolar
Tip of the tongue	Point after the teeth ridge		Post-alveolar
Curled tip of the tongue	Hard palate		Retroflex
Tip, blade and front of the tongue	Teeth ridge and hard palate		Palate-alveolar
Front of the tongue	Hard palate		Palatal
Back of the tongue	Soft palate		Velar
Back of the tongue	Uvula		Uvular
Back and root of the tongue	Pharynx		Pharyngeal
Glottis	Glottis		Glottal
Lower lip	Upper lip	Hard palate	Labio-palatal
Lower lip	Upper lip	Soft palate	Labio-velar

4.8.5 Manner of Articulation

In the previous section, we saw the places where the outgoing air encounters obstruction. There can also be different manners of the obstruction which can produce different kinds of consonant sounds. This is known as manner of articulation. Categories of manner of articulation are based on the size of the air passage during the production of the sound. We shall now look at the different kinds of manner in which the outgoing air is obstructed.

4.8.5.1 Complete Closure and Sudden Release

The outgoing air does not find it possible to escape because two organs of speech come in close and firm contact with each other. The air is held or compressed and then the two organs suddenly lose contact allowing the air to escape with plosion. This is known as the stricture of complete closure and sudden release. The sounds that are produced are known as plosive sounds. The articulation of such sounds involves three stages. The following diagram will make it clear.

In the first stage of articulation, there is complete closure of the air passage at some point. As a result the outgoing air cannot move further. In the second stage, it is held or compressed behind the point for some time. Finally, in the third stage the two organs of speech block the passage part suddenly and the air is released. This sudden release results in plosion. In all such cases the air is released through the mouth as the soft palate is raised blocking the nasal passage.

4.8.5.2 Complete Closure and Nasal Release

For some other sounds also two organs of speech come in contact in the same manner as they do for plosive sounds and stop the outgoing air at that point. However, it is only the oral passage that is blocked completely. For these sounds the soft palate is lowered so the air can escape through the nose producing nasal sounds. This manner is called complete closure and nasal release. Nasal sounds are said to be hybrid because of complete closure in the oral cavity but comparatively free passage of air through the nasal cavity.

4.8.5.3 Complete Closure and Slow or Gradual Release

For the production of some other consonant sounds also there is complete closure of the air passage. As a result of this the air is stopped behind the point of closure as it happens in the production of plosive sounds. But now the third stage is different. Instead of the two organs blocking the passage of air parting suddenly, they part gradually. The consonant sounds produced thus are called affricates. The release of the affricate sounds like a fricative.

4.8.5.4 Complete Closure and Lateral Release

In yet another situation the central oral tract is completely closed and the air is allowed to escape through either one side or both sides of the tongue. This manner of articulation is known as complete closure and lateral release and the sounds produced are called lateral sounds.

4.8.5.5 Intermittent Closure

As against these types of closure there may be intermittent closure of the air passage. This means that two organs of speech meet and part repeatedly. The active articulator strikes in passing against a passive articulator. This manner of articulation produces consonants known as flaps or trills. It was Henry Sweet who gave it the exactness of the sense in which it is now used.

4.8.5.6 Narrowing

In some other cases the air passage is not completely closed in any of the above manners but there is only a narrowing. As a result of this the outgoing air produces some friction. The resultant sounds are known as fricatives. Fricatives articulated with a wider and flatter channel shape are usually termed slit fricatives, though the actual shape of the channel differs from sound to sound. For example, English sounds /s/ and /z/ are articulated with wide, flat-shaped channel, and /θ/ and /ð/ are articulated with a narrower, slightly deeper channel shape. Plosives and fricatives are also known as obstruents.

4.8.5.7 Approximants

Sometimes two organs of speech do come close to each other but the outgoing air is not obstructed. The consonants produced by this manner of articulation are called approximants.

4.8.5.8 Semi-vowels

Air passage may not be blocked or narrowed so that the air passes freely. This manner of articulation produces sounds known as semi-vowels. A semi-vowel is produced by glide-like movements from a tongue position equivalent to one of the close vowels. They are called semi-vowel because in form they are like vowels but they perform the function of a consonant.

4.9 Aspiration

We have seen that some sounds are contrastive in nature because of the fact that one is accompanied by a 'h' sound and the other is not, that is one is aspirated and the other is unaspirated. In our examples from Urdu/Hindi we saw that words like 'baat' and 'bhaat' (talk, boiled rice) have contrastive sounds in the beginning. Aspiration, therefore, is one of the factors for describing consonants in these languages. This, however, is not a distinctive feature in English and Arabic and many other languages.

4.10 Consonant Length

Like vowels consonants can also be of various lengths. According to Ladefoged "it is the general rule of English that, other things being equal, syllable initial consonants are shorter than syllable final consonants". Also, syllable final voiceless consonants are longer than the corresponding voiced consonants. We have seen that vowels before voiceless consonants are shorter than those before voiced consonants.

4.11 Fortis and Lenis Consonants

Vowels, we have seen, can either be tense or lax. Consonants can either be fortis or lenis. Voiceless sounds are generally fortis and voiced sounds lenis. Fortis sounds are supposed to have a greater muscular tension and so have a longer duration than the lenis ones. We have already seen that voiced sounds are longer than the voiceless sounds.

4.12 Anticipatory Articulation

In English an articulator that is not necessarily involved in a given sound will nearly always start moving toward its position in the next sound in which it is the primary articulator. This phenomenon is known as anticipatory articulation. The position specified for a given sound is known as target position.

4.13 Secondary Articulation

A lesser degree of closure by two articulators not involved in the primary articulation is known as secondary articulation.

4.14 Gemination

Sometimes consonants and vowels are so long that they can be analyzed as double consonants and double vowels. This phenomenon is called gemination and the sounds are called geminates. In English geminate consonants can occur only across word boundaries or in a word which has two morphemes, for example, 'bad day' (word boundary) and 'unnerve' (two morphemes). Examples of gemination can also be found in Indian languages.

4.15 Vocoids and Contoids

We have seen in earlier sections how vowels and consonants are defined. They are different from each other on account of their general phonetic form as well as their function in a syllable structure. However, if we look at the phonological aspect we shall find that there is some overlapping. There are some consonants which perform the function of nucleus in a syllable. In terms of form also we find that some segments which are traditionally classified as consonants, like semi-vowels, have the formal features of a vowel but they never function as the nucleus of a syllable.

In order to overcome this ambiguity, K.L. Pike introduced two new terms, namely vocoids and non-vocoids or contoids. According to him, a vocoid is a segment with a stricture of open approximation, with or without a velic closure, and with central passage of the air-stream. All other sounds are contoids. He then used the terms syllabic for a segment representing a V element, that is the nucleus, of syllable structure and non-syllabic for a segment which represents the C element, that is the marginal elements of a syllable structure. Thus, there can be a syllabic vocoid, like the medial sound in 'one', a non-syllabic vocoid like the first segment of 'yes', a syllabic contoid such as /n/ in the second syllable of 'button', and a non-syllabic contoid such as the sounds at the beginning of the two syllables of 'button', /b/ and /t/. Pike also suggested that the terms vowels and consonants can be used as synonyms of syllabic vocoids and non-syllabic contoids. These are the most common categories that can be found in the languages used all over the world.

4.16 The International Phonetic Alphabet

A person who begins to learn a language cannot quite decide how to pronounce a word or how to represent the sounds of a word in writing. This is because of several factors. First, for example in English, the same letter is used for various sounds in writing. For example, the letter 's' is used for the 's' sound as in the word 'sound', for 'sh' as in the word 'sure', for the sound 'z' as in the word 'his' and so on. Second, again in English, sometimes one sound is represented by many letters. For example, the 'sh' sound is represented by the letters 'sh' in 'sure', 'ss' as in the word 'assure' , 'sh' as in the word 'ship', 'ti' as in the word 'examination' and so on. Sometimes a letter is not at all pronounced. For example, 'k' in 'know' remains silent. Similarly 'l' in 'calm' is not pronounced. In order to overcome this problem the International Phonetic Association has devised a set of symbols which will consistently and uniformly represent all the sounds of not only English but all languages. This is based on the principle of 'one sound one symbol, one symbol one sound'. This means that no sound can be represented by two symbols and no symbol can represent two sounds. Thus, the symbol 's' will always represent the 's' sound and the 's' sound will always be represented by the symbol 's'. This is called phonetic script and the symbols together are known as phonetic alphabet. Writing words in phonetic script is called phonetic transcription. This can be broad or phonemic and narrow or allophonic as mentioned earlier. The first, we have seen, is written within slant lines, that is, / / and the second within square brackets, that is, [ ]. Thus, the phonemic and allophonic transcriptions of the word 'kin' will be '/kin/' and '[kʰin]', respectively. This is so because the actual sound produced in the beginning of the word is 'pʰ' which is an allophone of the phoneme /p/ as we shall see in the next chapter.

The International Phonetic Alphabet (revised to 2005)

consonants (pulmonic)

	LABIAL		CORONAL				DORSAL				LARYNGEAL	
	Bilabial	Labio-dental	Dental	Alveolar	Palato-alveolar	Retroflex	Alveolo-palatal	Palatal	Velar	Uvular	Pharyngeal	Glottal
Nasal	m	ɱ		n		ɳ		ɲ	ŋ	ɴ		
Plosive	p b			t d		ʈ ɖ		c ɟ	k ɡ	q ɢ	ʡ	ʔ
Fricative	ɸ β	f v	θ ð	s z	ʃ ʒ	ʂ ʐ	ɕ ʑ	ç ʝ	x ɣ	χ ʁ	ħ ʕ	h ɦ
Approximant		ʋ		ɹ		ɻ		j	ɰ			
Tap, flap		ⱱ		ɾ		ɽ						
Trill	ʙ			r						ʀ	ʜ ʢ	
Lateral fricative				ɬ ɮ		ꞎ		ʎ̝	ʟ̝			
Lateral approximant				l		ɭ		ʎ	ʟ			
Lateral flap				ɺ		ɭ̆						

Where symbols appear in pairs, the one to the right represents a modally voiced consonant, except for murmured ɦ. Shaded areas denote articulations judged to be impossible. Light grey letters are unofficial extensions of the IPA.

consonants (non-pulmonic)

clicks	implosives	ejectives
ʘ Bilabial fricated	ɓ Bilabial	ʼ examples:
ǀ Laminal alveolar fricated ("dental")	ɗ Dental or alveolar	pʼ Bilabial
ǃ Apical (post)alveolar abrupt ("retroflex")	ᶑ Retroflex	tʼ Dental or alveolar
ǂ Laminal postalveolar abrupt ("palatal")	ʄ Palatal	kʼ Velar
ǁ Lateral alveolar fricated ("lateral")	ɠ Velar	tɬʼ Lateral affricate
ʞ Velar (back released)	ʛ Uvular	sʼ Alveolar fricative

consonants (co-articulated)

ʍ Voiceless labialized velar approximant

w Voiced labialized velar approximant

ɥ Voiced labialized palatal approximant

ɧ Simultaneous x and ʃ (existence disputed)

t͡ʃ k͡p Affricates and double articulations may be joined by a tie bar

brackets

//morphophonemic//

/phonemic/

[phonetic]

⟨orthographic⟩

vowels

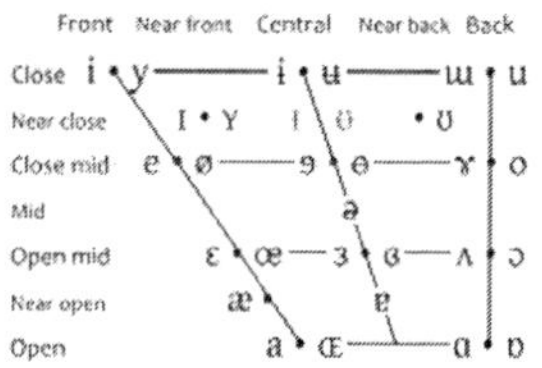

Vowels at right & left of bullets are rounded & unrounded.

suprasegmentals

ˈ	Primary stress	ˈˈ	Extra stress
ˌ	Secondary stress	[ˌfoʊnəˈtɪʃən]	
eː	Long	eˑ	Half-long
e	Short	ĕ	Extra-short
.	Syllable break	t‿a	Linking (no break)

intonation

|	Minor (foot) break		
‖	Major (intonation) break		
↗	Global rise	↘	Global fall

(tone)

level tones			*contour tones (e.g.)*		
e̋	˥	Top	ě	˩˥	Rising
é	˦	High	ê	˥˩	Falling
ē	˧	Mid	e᷄	˦˥	High rising
è	˨	Low	e᷅	˩˨	Low rising
ȅ	˩	Bottom	e᷇	˥˦	High falling
tone terracing			e᷆	˨˩	Low falling
ꜛ		Upstep	e᷈	˧˦˧	Peaking
ꜜ		Downstep	e᷉	˧˨˧	Dipping

diacritics

Diacritics may be moved to fit a letter, as ŋ̊ or ɟ̊. Other letters may be used as diacritics of phonetic detail: tˢ (fricative release), bʱ (breathy voice), mˀ (glottalized), ᵊ (epenthetic schwa), oʷ (off-glide), ɯᵝ (compressed).

SYLLABICITY & RELEASES		PHONATION		PRIMARY ARTICULATION		SECONDARY ARTICULATION			
ŋ̍ ɹ̩	Syllabic	n̥ d̥	Voiceless or Slack voice	t̪ b̪	Dental	tʷ dʷ	Labialized	ɔ̹ χ̹	More rounded
e̯ ʊ̯	Non-syllabic	s̬ d̬	Modal voice or Stiff voice	t̺ d̺	Apical	tʲ dʲ	Palatalized	ɔ̜ χʷ̜	Less rounded
tʰ ʰt	(Pre)aspirated	n̤ a̤	Breathy voice	t̻ d̻	Laminal	tˠ dˠ	Velarized	ẽ z̃	Nasalized
dⁿ	Nasal release	n̰ a̰	Creaky voice	u̟ t̟	Advanced	tˤ dˤ	Pharyngealized	ɚ ɝ	Rhoticity
dˡ	Lateral release	n͈ a͈	Strident	i̠ t̠	Retracted	ɫ z̴	Velarized or pharyngealized	e̘ o̘	Advanced tongue root
t̚	No audible release	n̼ d̼	Linguolabial	ä ÿ	Centralized	ɯ̽	Mid-centralized	e̙ o̙	Retracted tongue root
e̞ β̞	Lowered (β̞ is a bilabial approximant)			e̝ ɹ̝	Raised (ɹ̝ is a voiced alveolar non-sibilant fricative, r̝ a fricative trill)				

Exercise

1. What are vowels? Answer with suitable examples.
2. Discuss the cardinal vowel scale. What is the significance of the cardinal vowel scale?
3. What is a diphthong? Discuss the different types of diphthong and give appropriate examples.
4. What factors are responsible for vowel quality? Exemplify.
5. Discuss the factors responsible for determining the vowel length.
6. How are vowels different from consonants? Give examples.
7. Discuss the factors that are taken into consideration in order to classify and describe the consonants.
8. Discuss the places and manners of articulation of the consonants.
9. Write a note on anticipatory articulation and co-articulation.
10. What are vocoids and contoids? How are they different from vowels and consonants?
11. How is International Phonetic Alphabet different from the alphabet of a language? Give examples.

5

The Sounds of English

English has a stock of forty-four distinctive sounds which are used in different permutations and combinations to form all the words of the language. Out of these forty-four sounds, twenty are vowels and the remaining twenty-four are consonants. We shall now see how these sounds are produced, classified and described as the different allophones of a phoneme, that is, the distinctive sound. We must, however, remember that like any other language English is also spoken in many different ways by its speakers in different regions of the world. For example, the way it is spoken in the U.S.A. is different from the way it is spoken in England. In England also it is not spoken in the same way throughout the country. Here we are concerned with the spoken English of the southern England which is popularly known as the Received Pronunciation or R.P. This variety is regarded as the standard variety we hear on the radio, T.V. and at official conferences, seminars, etc. It may, however, be noted that this variety does not enjoy the same status now as it did earlier because of the fact that people's mobility has increased manifold as a result of growth in the modes of travel. This has resulted into the emergence of modified R.P. or rather modified R.Ps. Then there is also the Estuary English along the river Thames. But for the purpose of teaching and learning English this R.P. still serves as the model. So the description here will follow the original R.P. model. The symbols used are those which

Gimson has used. We shall first look at the vowels and then at the consonants.

5.1 Vowels of English

Of the twenty vowel sounds, twelve are pure vowels and the remaining eight are vowel glides or diphthongs.

5.1.1 Pure Vowels

All those vowels which occur as a single distinct identifiable unit in a syllable are pure vowels. Let us see all these pure vowels.

(I) /i:/ as in eat, beat, bee, etc.

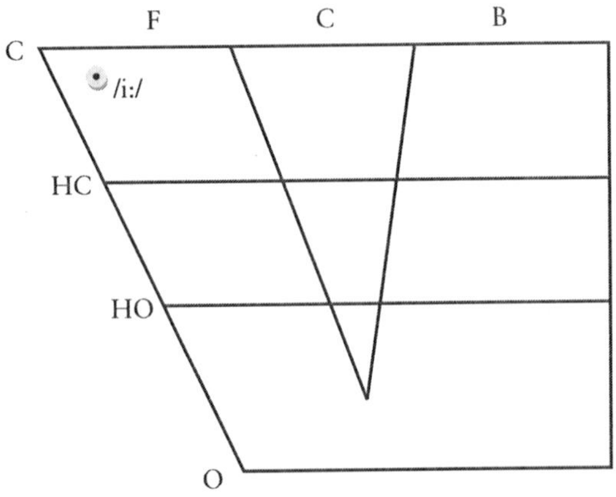

Here we find that this vowel is produced when the front of the tongue is raised up to almost the highest permissible point for the production of a vowel. Again, when we speak the words in the examples above, we find that the lips are spread or unrounded. This vowel can, therefore, be described as the front nearly close unrounded vowel. It is a tense vowel.

Distribution

It occurs initially, medially and finally as in the examples above.

Spelling

In writing, it is realized by the letter 'e' as in the word 'complete', 'ee' as in 'bee', 'ea' as in 'feat', 'ei' as in 'conceive', 'i' as in 'competition', 'oe' as in 'foetus', 'ey' as in 'key', 'uay' as in 'quay', 'ae' as in 'aesthetics', etc.

(II) /ɪ/ as in it, bit, hurry, etc. In this vowel also, the front of the tongue is raised towards the hard palate but it goes up to a point just above the half close position. Like the previous vowel this vowel is also spoken with unrounded lips. This vowel can, therefore, be described as the front half close unrounded vowel. This is a lax vowel.

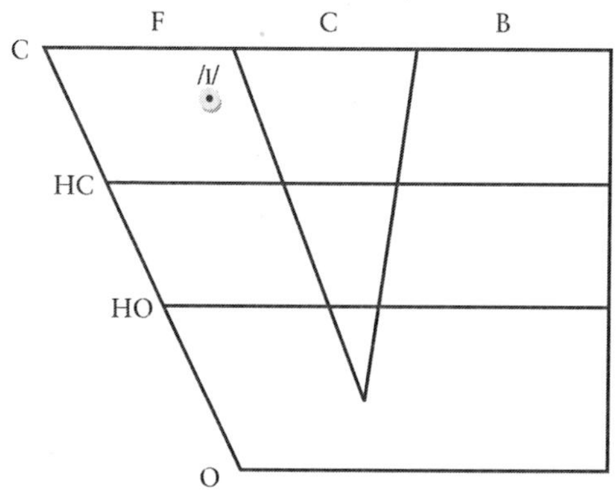

Distribution

This vowel also occurs initially, medially and finally as in the above examples.

Spelling

In writing, it is realized by 'i' as in 'it', 'e' as in 'competition', 'y' as in 'hurry', 'a' as in 'village', 'ui' as in 'build', 'o' as in 'women', 'ia' as in 'marriage', 'ai' as in 'bargain', 'ie' as in 'carried', 'u' as in 'busy', 'ey' as in 'bailey', 'ae' as in 'praesidium', etc.

Daniel Jones found that the front of the tongue is raised a little higher for the articulation of this vowel. So he used another symbol /i/ that is a lower case 'I' without two dots that we find for the previous vowel. According to him, the difference between this vowel and the previous one is only in length. Later A.C. Gimson changed the symbol to /i/ because for him these two vowels differed not only in length but also in quality. In the description of Jones this vowel occurs a little higher than what we find in Gimson's description. Also in Gimson's description this vowel occurs a little towards the centre but in Jones's description it is fronter.

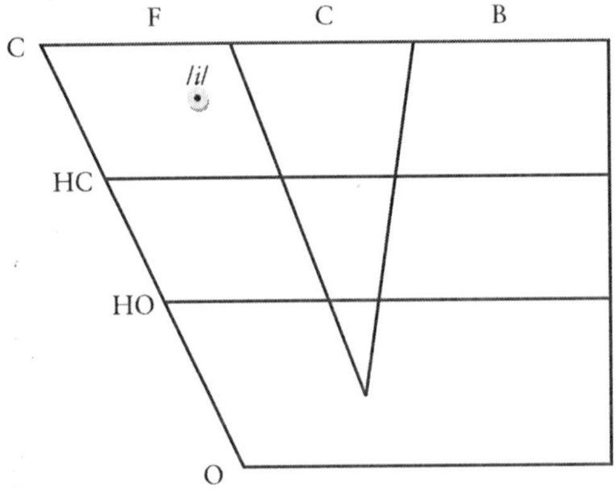

As shown by Jones

(III) /e/ as in ate, bet, etc. For the production of this vowel also the front of the tongue is used, but it is now raised to a point which is almost between half open and half close points. The lips are again unrounded. This vowel, therefore, is front between half open and half close position and unrounded. It is a lax vowel.

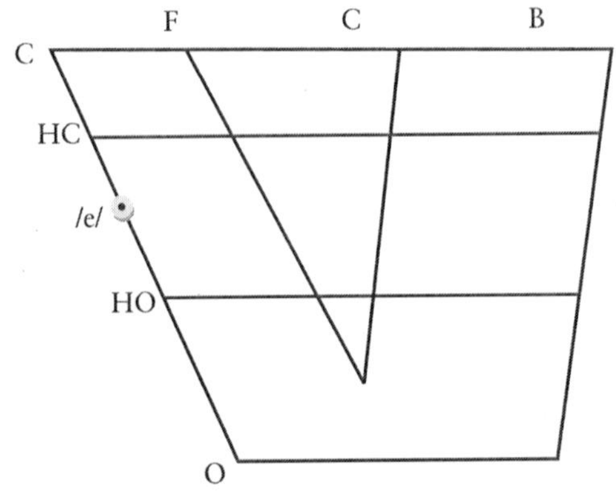

Distribution

This vowel occurs only initially and medially. It does not occur finally.

Spelling

In writing, it is realized by the letter 'e' as in 'bet', 'a' as in 'ate', 'u' as in 'bury', 'ei' as in 'leisure', 'ai' as in 'said', 'ea' as in 'measure', 'ie' as in 'friend', etc.

(IV) /æ/ as in at, bat, etc. This vowel is also produced by the front of the tongue. It is raised to a point between half open and open positions and the lips are unrounded. It is described as front between half open and open unrounded vowel and like the previous vowel it is lax.

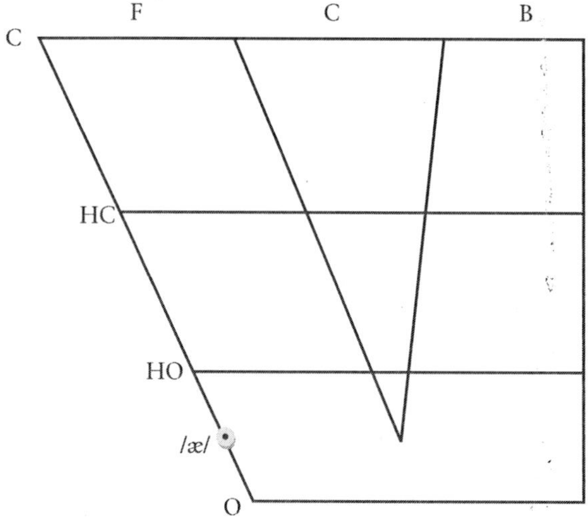

Distribution

Like the previous vowel this vowel also occurs only initially and medially and does not occur finally.

Spelling

In writing, it is realized by the letter 'a' as in the above examples.

(V) /ɑ:/ as in art, fast, far, etc. For the production of this vowel it is the back of the tongue which is used. It lies at the open position and the lips are unrounded. The vowel, therefore, is back open unrounded.

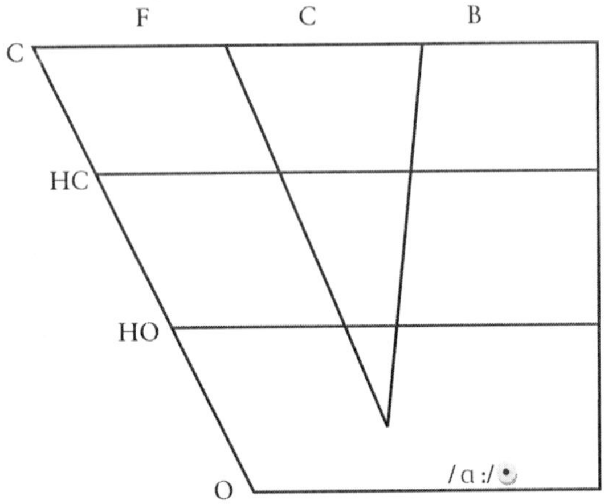

Distribution

This vowel occurs initially, medially and finally as in the examples above. It should be noted that 'r' as in 'far' is not pronounced in R.P.

Spelling

In writing, it is realized by the letters 'ar' as in 'jar', 'a' as in 'last', 'e+r' as in 'clerk', 'ea+r' as in 'heart', 'au' as in 'laugh'.

(VI) /ɒ/ as in of, cot, etc. For the production of this vowel it is again the back of the tongue which is used. It is raised to a point between open and half open positions and the lips are unrounded. This vowel can be described as back between open and half open unrounded vowel.

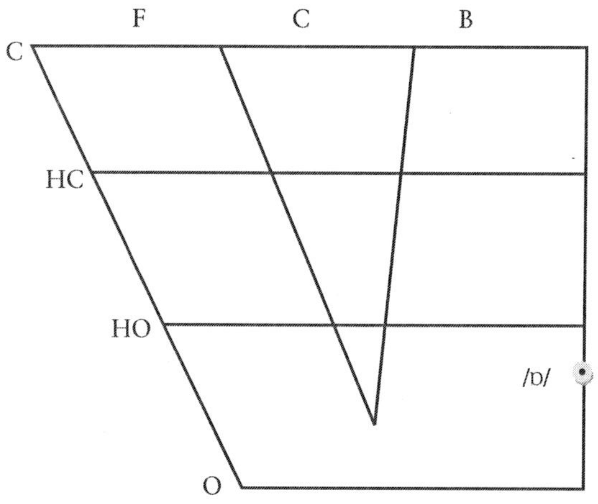

Distribution

It occurs initially and medially but not finally.

Spelling

In writing, it is realized by the letter 'o' as in 'of', 'o+r' as in 'moral', 'u+a' as in 'quality', 'au' as in 'because', 'ou' as in 'cough', 'e' as in 'ennui', etc.

For this vowel Daniel Jones found that the tongue is raised a little higher than the position assigned by A.C. Gimson who found it to be a little lower with greater jaw opening. Jones used the symbol / /.

(VII) /ɔ:/ as in all, fall, law, etc. For the production of this vowel the back of the tongue is raised to a point between half open and half close positions and the lips are now rounded. Therefore, this vowel is a back between half open and half close rounded vowel.

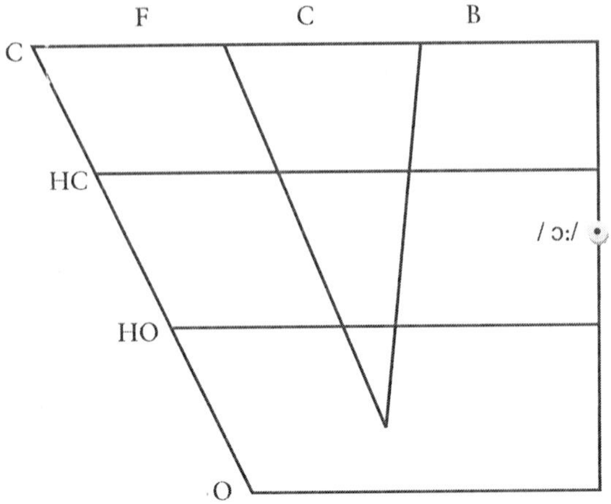

Distribution

This vowel occurs initially, medially and finally as in the examples above.

Spelling

In writing, it is realized by the letter ‘a’ as in ‘all’, ‘aw’ as in ‘law’, ‘ou’ as in ‘ought’, ‘al’ as in ‘chalk’, ‘w+ar’ as in ‘towards’, ‘o+ar’ as in ‘board’, ‘o+r’ as in ‘forward’, ‘oo+r’ as in ‘door’, ‘au’ as in ‘fraud’, etc.

Daniel Jones found this vowel to be at the half open position but he used the same symbol.

(VIII) /ʊ/ as in cook, foot, etc. This vowel is produced when the back of the tongue is raised to a point just above the half close position and the lips are rounded. It is, therefore a back nearly half close rounded vowel. It is a lax vowel.

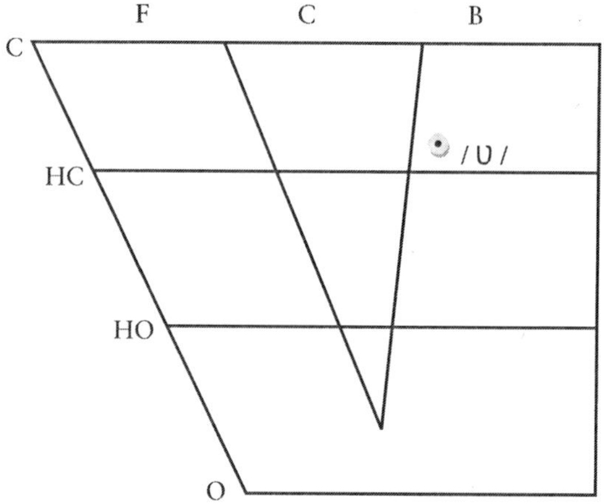

Distribution

The maximum occurrence of this vowel is found to be in the medial position. Initially it occurs in a word like 'umlaut' and finally in the weak form of the preposition 'to'.

Spelling

In spelling, it is realized by 'u' as in 'put', 'o' as in 'woman', 'oo' as in 'book', 'ou' as in 'could', 'ui' as in 'cruise', etc.

Daniel Jones assigned this vowel a position above the position assigned by A.C. Gimson and also found it to be backer. He used the symbol /u/ for this vowel. For him the difference between this vowel and the next one was that of length only but Gimson thought that it was of quality. So he assigned another symbol.

(IX) /u:/ as in use, boot, sue, etc. For this vowel it is the back of the tongue which is raised and it is raised to a point almost near the close position. The lips are again rounded. This vowel can be described as back almost close rounded vowel. It is a tense vowel.

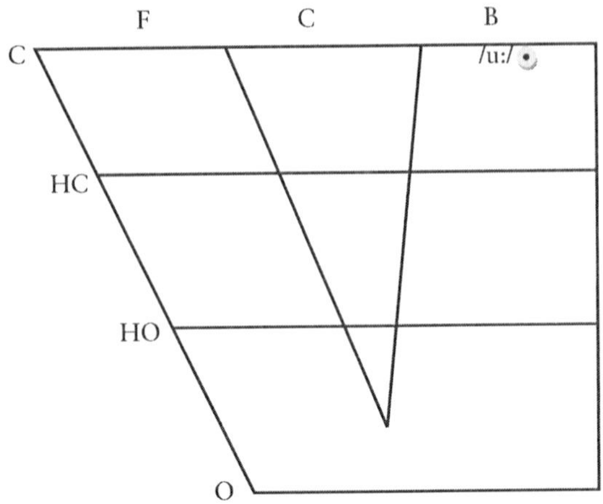

Distribution

This vowel occurs initially, medially and finally as in the examples above.

Spelling

In spelling, it is realized by the letter 'u' as in 'use', 'oo' as in 'boot', 'ou' as in 'group', 'ui' as in 'fruit', 'ew' as in 'few', 'eau' as in 'beauty', 'oe' as in 'shoe', 'wo' as in 'two', 'o' as in 'to', 'ue' as in 'blue', 'oeu' as in 'manoeuvre', etc.

(X) /ɜ:/ as in early, bird, etc. For the articulation of this vowel it is the centre of the tongue which is used. It is raised to a point between half open and half close positions and the lips are unrounded. It is a central between half open and half close unrounded vowel and is lax.

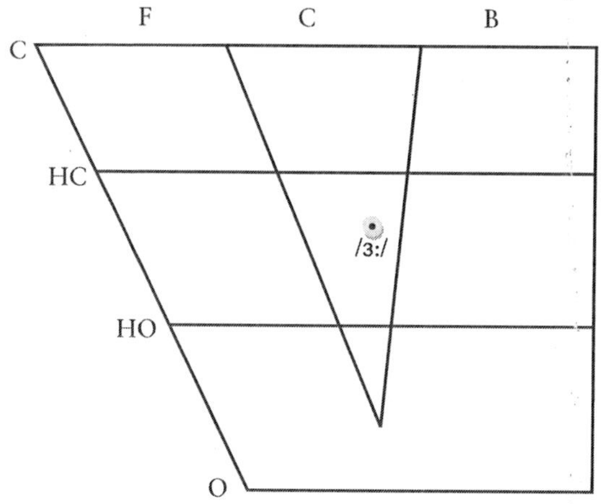

Distribution

This vowel also occurs initially, medially and finally as in the examples above.

Spelling

In writing, it is realized by the letters 'ea+r' as in 'early', 'e+r' as in 'herd', 'i+r' as in 'bird', 'u+r' as in 'hurt', 'o+r' as in 'word', 'our' as in 'journey', etc.

(XI) /ə/ this vowel is articulated in two different ways in the non-final and final positions.

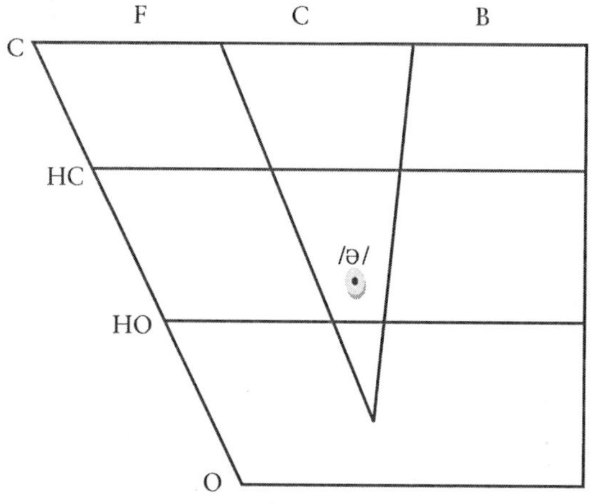

Non-final as in about, admiral, etc. In this position the centre of the tongue is raised to a point between half open and half close positions and the lips are unrounded. So in this position it is a central between half open and half close unrounded vowel.

Final as in father, mother, etc. In this position the centre of the tongue is raised to the half open point and the lips are again unrounded. So it is a central half open unrounded vowel. In both positions it is lax.

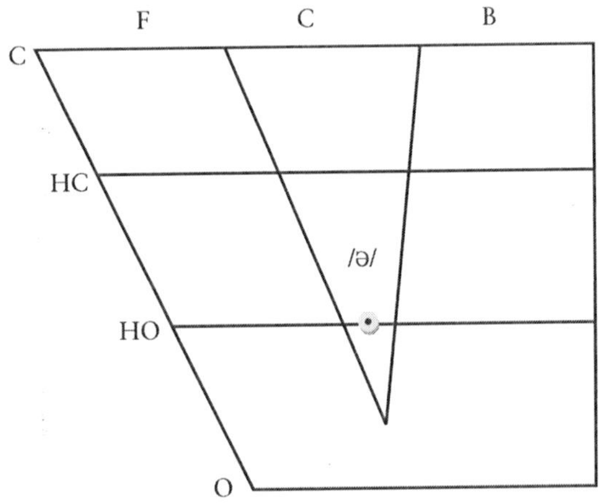

Distribution

Together they occur initially, medially and finally as in the examples above.

Spelling

In spelling, it is realized by the letter 'a' as in 'above', 'ar' as in 'forward', 'e' as in 'problem', 'e+r' as in 'liberty', 'i' as in 'terrible', 'o' as in 'condition', 'o+r' as in 'effort', 'ou' as in 'colour', 'u' as in 'succeed', 'u+r' as in 'surprise', 'ue' as in 'masquerade', 'ua' as in 'mortuary', 'a+r' as in 'far', etc.

This vowel is also known as the neutral vowel or schwa. It never occurs in a stressed syllable.

(XII) /ʌ/ as in up, cup, etc. For this vowel the centre of the tongue is raised to a point between open and half open positions and the lips are unrounded. It is therefore, a central between open and half open unrounded vowel and is lax.

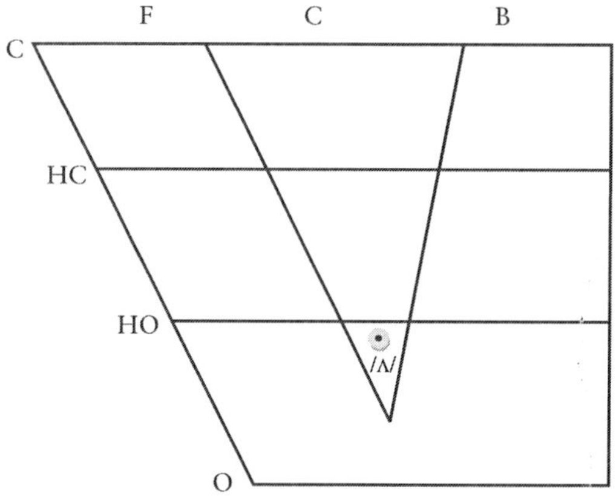

Distribution

It occurs initially and medially as in the examples above but does not occur finally.

Spelling

In writing, it is realized by the letter 'u' as in 'up', 'o' as in 'borough', 'oo' as in 'flood', etc.

All of these 12 pure vowels may be seen in the following diagram.

The Pure Vowels of English (RP)

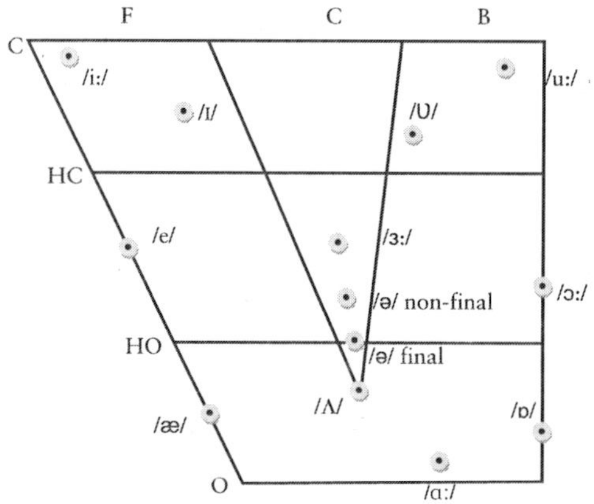

5.1.2 *The Pure Vowels in the Speech of Indian Speakers of English*

English is spoken in many different ways in different regions of India. A variety of English acceptable throughout the country has, however, been evolved and is known as General Indian English or G.I.E. for short. This differs from R.P. in some respects. The following diagram will make the difference in the articulation of pure vowels clear.

The Pure Vowels in Indian English

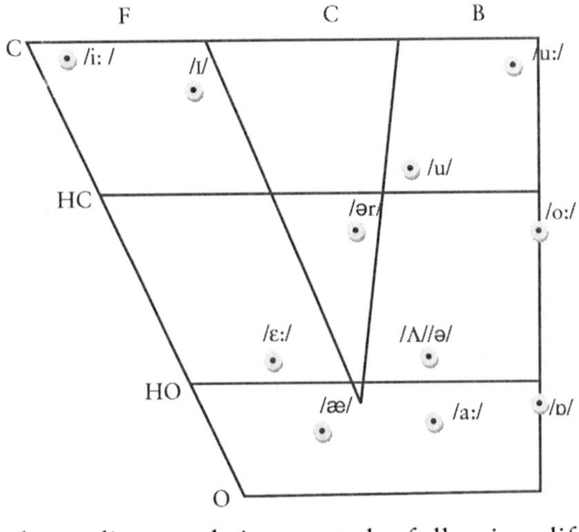

The above diagram brings out the following differences:

(a) The vowel /i/ is closer and fronter in Indian English.

(b) /ɛ/ is opener and retracted than R.P. /e/.

(c) /æ/ is also slightly opener and retracted than R.P. /æ/.

(d) /a:/ is somewhat centralized and less open than R.P. /ɑ:/.

(e) /ɒ/ is slightly opener and fronter than R.P. (Gimson)

(f) /ʊ/ is closer and backer than R.P. /ɒ/. (Gimson)

(g) /ər/ replaces R.P. /ɜ:/ as in 'journey'.

(h) R.P. /ʌ/ is realized as both /ə/ and /ʌ/ but Indian English /ʌ/ is backer than R.P. /ʌ/.

(i) R.P. /ɔ:/ is not found in Indian English.

5.1.3 Diphthongs or Glides

A diphthong is a vowel glide as we find that one vowel sound glides towards another vowel sound within a syllable. English (R.P.) has eight diphthongs or glides as we have seen. We know that a diphthong has two elements. Therefore in order to describe a diphthong both the elements are taken into consideration. Let us now have a look at the diphthongs of English.

(I) /eɪ/ as in eight, late, lay, etc. For the production of this vowel the front of the tongue moves from the point of pure vowel /e/ towards the point of pure vowel /ɪ/. The first element is front between half open and half close unrounded and the second element is front between half open and half close unrounded.

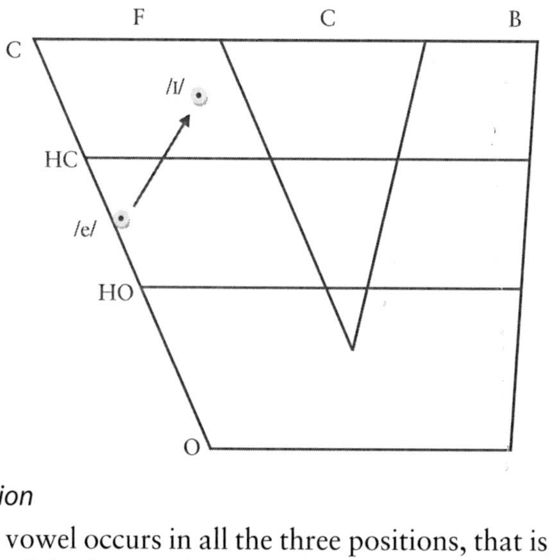

Distribution

This vowel occurs in all the three positions, that is, initial, medial and final as in the examples above.

Spelling

In writing, it is realized by the letter 'a' as in 'gate', 'ay' as in 'ray', 'ai' as in 'aim', 'ei' as in 'eight', 'ey' as in 'whey', 'ea' as in 'great', 'ee' as in 'matinee', 'ue' as in 'bouquet', 'ae' as in 'blaeberry', etc.

(II) /aɪ/ as in icon, light, shy, etc. For the articulation of this diphthong the tongue moves from the point of the pure vowel /a/ which is front and open towards that of /ɪ/ which is front and nearly half close. The lips are unrounded for both.

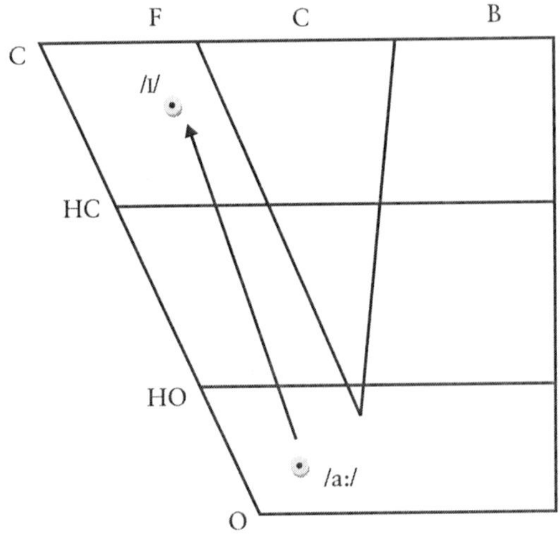

Distribution

This vowel also occurs initially, medially and finally as in the examples above.

Spelling

In spelling, it is realized by 'i+gh' as in 'light', 'y' as in 'shy', 'ie' as in 'vie', 'ei' as in 'height', 'uy' as in 'buy', 'ey' as in 'eye', etc.

(III) /ɔɪ/ as in oil, choice, joy, etc. The first element is back between open and half open points and the lips are rounded and the second element is front nearly half close unrounded.

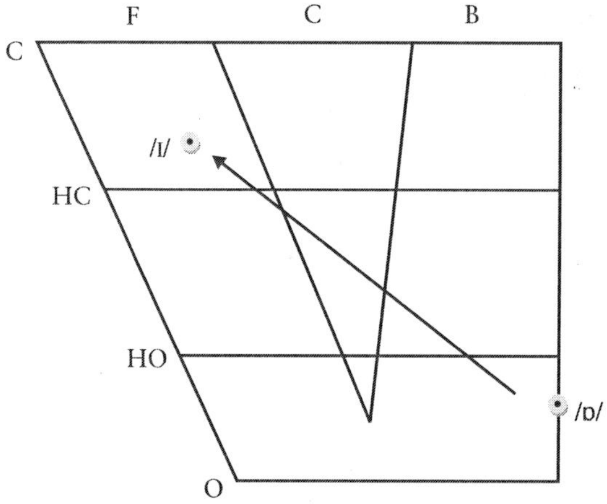

Distribution

This diphthong also occurs in all the three positions, that is, initial, medial and final as in the examples above.

Spelling

In writing, it is realized by the letters 'oi' as in 'oil', 'oy' as in 'joy', etc.

(IV) /əU/ as in old, gold, so, etc. For this diphthong the first element is central between half close and half open unrounded and the second element is back between half close and close rounded.

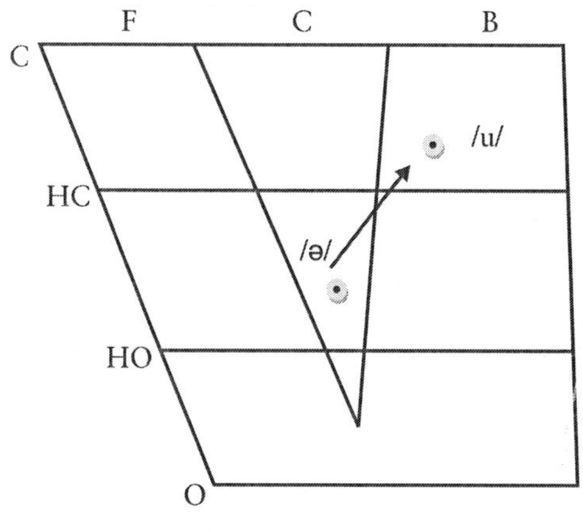

Distribution

Like the previous vowel it occurs initially, medially and finally as in the examples above.

Spelling

In writing, it is realized by the letter 'o' as in 'old', 'ou' as in 'shoulder', 'oa' as in 'moan', 'ou' as in 'mourn', 'o+cc' as in 'occult', 'au' as in 'mauve', etc.

(V) /aʊ/ as in out, bout, how, etc. The first element is back open unrounded and the second back nearly half close rounded.

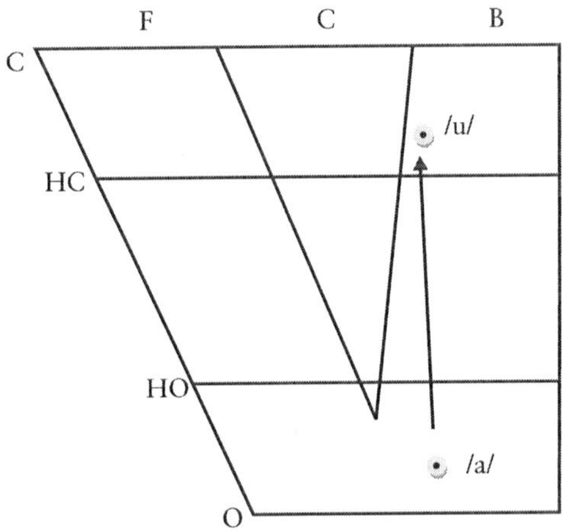

Distribution

This vowel also occurs initially, medially and finally as in the examples above.

Spelling

In writing, it is realized by 'ou' as in 'out', 'au' as in 'drought', 'ow' as in 'now', etc.

(VI) /ɪə/ as in ear, material, fear, etc. For this diphthong the first element is front slightly above the half close position and the second element is central half open and both are unrounded.

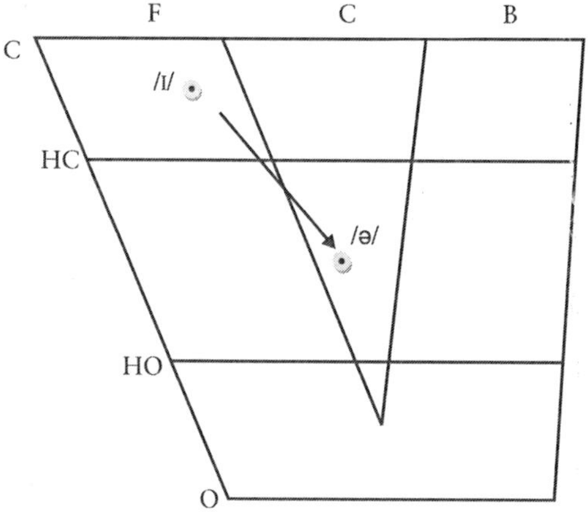

Distribution

It occurs initially, medially and finally as in the examples above.

Spelling

In writing, it is realized by the letters 'ea' as in 'ear', 'e' as in 'zero', 'ee' as in 'cheer', 'ie' as in 'tier', 'ere' as in 'atmosphere', 'ei' as in 'weird', 'ia' as in 'arial', 'eo' as in 'pleonasm', etc.

(VII) /eə/ as in air, chair, etc. The first element is front between half close and half open and the second element is central between half open and half close and both are unrounded.

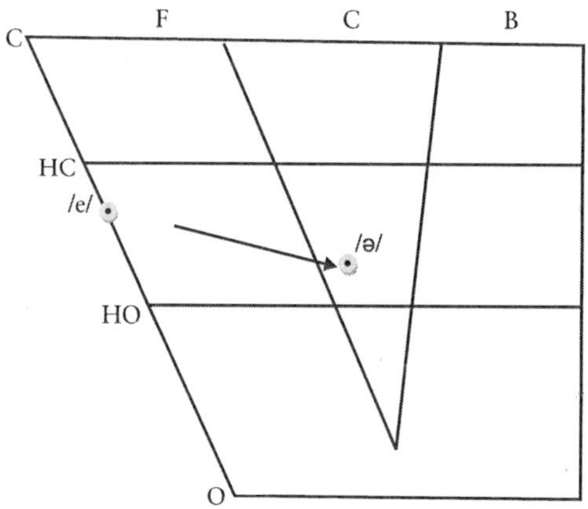

Distribution

It occurs initially and finally as in the examples above.

Spelling

In writing, it is realized by the letters 'ai+r' as in 'air', 'a+r' as in 'fare', 'ea' as in 'bear', 'ae' as in 'aeroplane', 'ei' as in 'their', 'e' as in 'there', etc.

(VIII) /ʊə/ as in moor, tourist, etc. The first element for this diphthong is back nearly half close rounded and the second element is central between half close and half open unrounded.

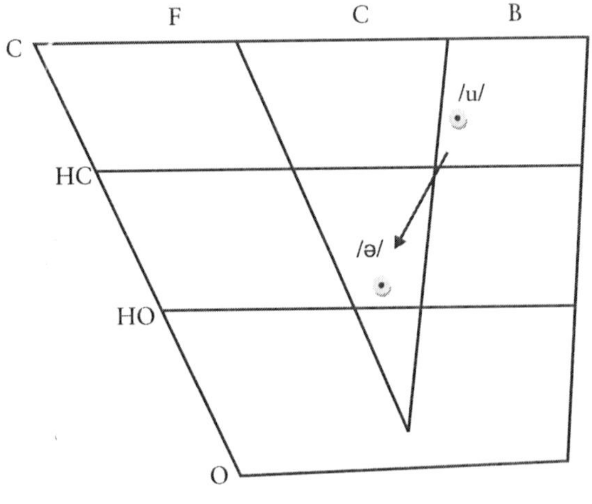

Distribution

This vowel occurs medially and finally as in the examples above.

Spelling

In writing, it is realized by the letters 'oo' as in 'moor', 'ou' as in 'tour', 'u+r' as in 'sure', 'eu' as in 'pleurisy', etc.

5.1.4 Difference in the Descriptions of Jones and Gimson

As in the case of pure vowels, Daniel Jones' description of diphthongs differs from that of A.C. Gimson in some respects. The following diagram will bring out the differences.

Diphthongs of English (RP)

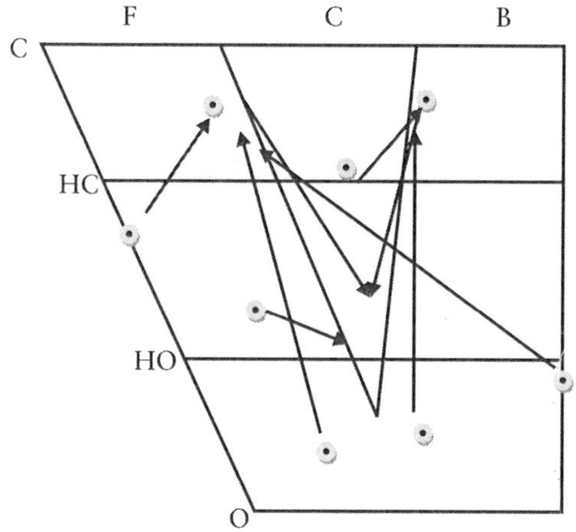

A.C. Gimson

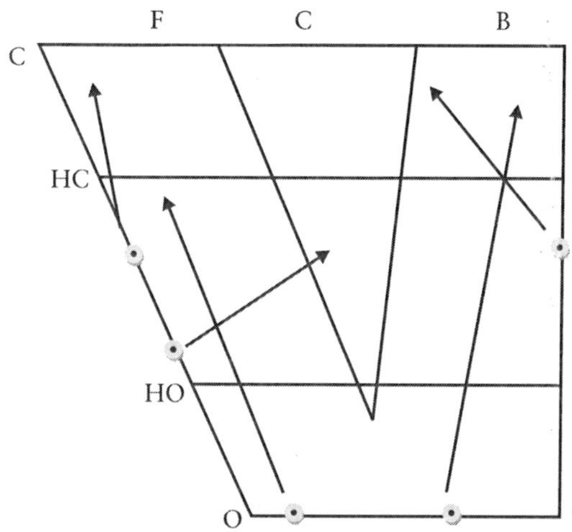

Daniel Jones

The above diagrams show the following differences.

(a) /eɪ/: In Jones' description the second element is closer and fronter.

(b) /aɪ/: Both elements are fronter in the description given by Jones.

(c) /eə/: In Jones' description the first element is fronter and opener and the second element is opener.

(d) /aʊ/: Jones' description places the first element a little retracted and the second element closer and backer. He uses the symbol /ɒu/.

(e) /əʊ/: Daniel Jones found the first element to be back between half open and half close positions and the second element closer and used the symbol /ou/ for this vowel.

5.1.5 Diphthongs in the Speech of Indian Speakers

Like the pure vowels diphthongs are also not articulated by the Indian speakers in the same way as they are done by R.P. speakers. The following chart will bring out the differences.

Diphthongs in Indian English

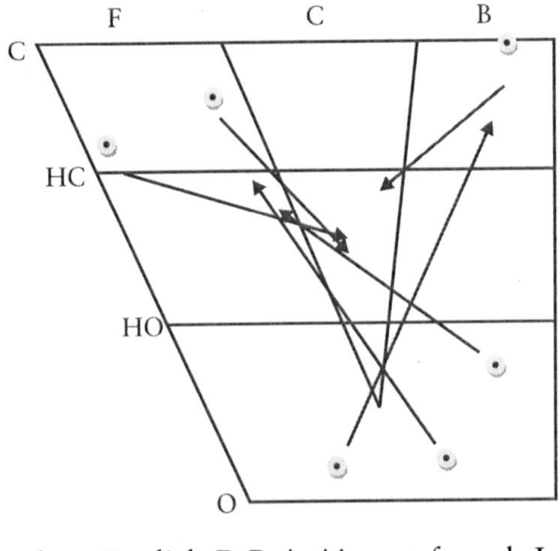

(a) In Indian English R.P. /əɪ/ is not found. It is replaced by a long pure vowel /e:/.

(b) In Indian English the first element of the diphthong /aɪ/ is back and less open and the second element is centralized between half close and half open positions.

(c) In Indian English the first element of the diphthong /ɔɪ/ is somewhat fronted and opener and the lips are less rounded. The second element is also opener. The symbol given is /ɔɪ/.

(d) The R.P. diphthong /əʊ/ is not found in Indian English. Instead a long pure vowel /o:/ is used.

(e) The first element of R.P. /aʊ/ is less open and fronted and the second element is back but retracted. The symbol used is /au/.

(f) Both elements of R.P. /ɪə/, /eə/ and /ʊə/ are closer in Indian English.

5.1.6 Facts about Diphthongs

The above description brings out the following facts about diphthongs.

5.1.6.1 *Length and Glide*: The length of the diphthong is associated with the first element in a falling diphthong. In a rising diphthong it is the second element which has a greater length.

Another feature of a glide is that its length is equivalent to that of a long pure vowel. Its reduced form shows shortening.

5.1.6.2 Another interesting fact about the diphthongs is that the first elements are generally in the region of /ɪ/, /eɪ/, /a/, /ɑ/, /ə/ and /ʊ/ and the second in the region of /ɪ/, /ə/ and /ʊ/.

5.1.6.3 In English no diphthong occurs before the velar nasal /ŋ/ unless word final alveolar nasal /n/ is assimilated to [ŋ].

5.2 Consonants of English

Consonants, we have seen, are speech sounds which are produced when there is some obstruction or narrowing in the vocal tract which results in audible friction. We have also seen that consonants can be classified and described on the basis of the following considerations:

(a) Air stream

(b) Position of the soft palate

(c) State of the glottis

(d) Place of articulation

(e) Manner of articulation

(f) Aspiration.

However, (i) since all English sounds are produced by the same air-stream, that is, pulmonic egressive air-stream, (ii) all but three consonants are oral and (iii) aspiration is not a distinctive feature in English, in describing the consonants of English we shall take into consideration only (i) the state of the glottis, (ii) place of articulation and (iii) manner of articulation. This will give us three-term labels for these sounds. English, we have seen earlier, has twenty-four consonants and depending on their phonetic environment or context, they have their allophones. Let us now look at these consonants and their allophones.

5.2.1 Plosives

There are three pairs /p,b/, /t,d/ and /k,g/ of plosives in English. /p/ as in pit, spit, sip, etc. For the production of this sound vocal cords (glottis) are wide apart, so there is no vibration and the sound is voiceless. This sound is produced when the lower lip comes in close and firm contact with the upper lip, so the sound is bilabial. The contact is maintained for some time and then the lips are suddenly parted allowing the air to escape with plosion. It is thus a plosive sound. This can be described as voiceless bilabial plosive. It is a fortis sound as it is pronounced with more force than /b/ that is its counterpart.

Allophones

The following are the allophones of this phoneme.

(a) Aspirated [ph] as in pit, pray, etc. The /p/ here is pronounced in such a way that vibration for the following vowel sound is delayed and this delay is filled with the sound of the expulsion of a puff of air or aspiration. This happens when /p/ occurs in the beginning of a stressed syllable, that is, at the stressed initial position in a syllable.

(b) Unaspirated [p] as in spit. When /p/ is preceded by another sound, chiefly /s/, aspiration does not take place even if it occurs in a stressed syllable as in the example above.

(c) Unexploded [p] as in cap. This allophone occurs when /p/ is in the final position as in the example above.

(d) Nasally released [p] as in topmost when it is followed by a homorganic nasal sound. Two sounds are homorganic if their place of articulation is the same such as /p/ and /m/.

(e) Lip rounded [p] as in pool when the next sound is a rounded vowel as in the examples above.

(f) Lip spread [p] as in peel when the next sound is an unrounded vowel as in the example above.

Distribution

It occurs initially, medially and finally as in the examples above.

Spelling

In writing, it is realized by the letter 'p', 'pp' as in 'peal' and 'appeal', etc. The letter 'p' is not pronounced when it is followed by either 'n' or 's' in the beginning of a word, for example, in 'pneumatic', 'psalm', 'psephologist', 'psychology', etc. The letter 'p' followed by 'h' also remains silent in the word 'phthysis'. In the word 'cupboard' it gets assimilated to the following /b/ sound. It also remains silent when followed by 't' in the beginning of a word as in 'ptarmigan', 'ptomaine', etc.

/b/ as in bit, above, rob, etc. The only difference between this consonant and the previous one is that for the articulation of this sound the vocal cords are loosely held together while they are wide apart for the previous one. This consonant is, therefore, voiced. In respect of place and manner of articulation it is like /p/. So it is a voiced bilabial plosive. It is also called lenis as it is pronounced with less force than its counterpart /p/.

Allophones

This consonant has the following allophones.

(a) Unexploded [b] as in rob, (b) nasally exploded [b] as in submit, (c) devoiced [b] in the final position as in rob, (d) lip rounded [b] when followed by a rounded vowel as in book, (e) lip spread [b] when followed by an unrounded vowel as in bee and (f) laterally released [b] when followed by the lateral sound as in blog.

Distribution

This consonant also occurs in all the three positions as in the examples above.

Spelling

In writing, it is realized by the letter 'b' as in 'bit', 'bb' as in 'robbing', etc. The letter 'b' is not pronounced when it is preceded by 'm' as in words like 'comb', 'tomb', etc. It is not pronounced in words such as 'subtle', 'debt', etc.

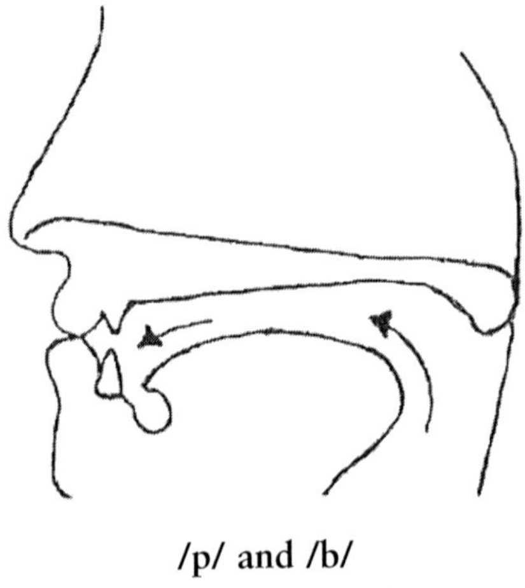

/p/ and /b/

/t/ as in tip, stop, rot, etc. For the articulation of this sound vocal cords are wide apart and so they do not vibrate. It is, therefore, voiceless and fortis. The tip of the tongue comes in close and firm contact with the alveolar ridge. So it is an alveolar sound. The contact is removed suddenly and the compressed air is expelled with plosion. It is, therefore, a plosive sound. /t/ is thus a voiceless alveolar plosive.

Allophones

It has the following allophones.

(a) Aspirated [th] in stressed initial position as in 'tin', (b) unaspirated [t] when it occurs in unstressed syllables and when preceded by 's' as in 'practical' and 'stop', (c) unexploded [t] in the final position as in 'rot', (d) nasally released [t] when followed by a homorganic nasal sound as in the word 'witness', (e) laterally released [t] when followed by a lateral sound as in 'outlet', (f) lip rounded [t] when followed by a rounded vowel as in the word 'stool', (g) lip spread [t] when followed by an unrounded vowel as in 'team' and (h) post-alveolar [t] when followed by a post-alveolar sound as in 'trip'.

Distribution

This consonant also occurs in all the three positions. However, native speakers of English usually use the glottal stop in place of /t/ when it occurs in the medial and final positions.

Spelling

In writing, it is realized by the letter 't' as in 'top', 'tt' as in 'attract', 'd' as in 'walked'. (When a verb ends in 'd' or 'ed' and the previous sound is voiceless other than /t/, the past ending has the sound /t/.)

The letter 't' remains silent when followed by 's' as in words like 'Tsar', 'Tsarina', etc. It also remains silent in words like fasten, often, hasten, bouquet, postpone, etc.

/d/ as in door, adore, rode, etc. The difference in the articulation of /t/ and /d/ is the same as that for the articulation of /p/ and /b/. While for /t/ there is no vibration for /d/ there is vibration because the vocal cords are loosely held together. In respect of place and manner of articulation they are identical. It is, therefore, voiced alveolar plosive. It is a lenis sound.

Allophones

Like /b/ it is never aspirated. It has the following allophones. (a) Unexploded when in the final position as in ride, (b) devoiced, again in the final position, as in ride, (c) nasally released when followed by a homorganic nasal sound as in 'bad news', (d) laterally released when followed by a lateral sound as in 'bed lamp', (e) lip rounded when followed by a rounded vowel as in 'dome', (f) lip spread when followed by an unrounded vowel as in 'dim' and (g) post-alveolar when followed by a post-alveolar sound as in 'drip'.

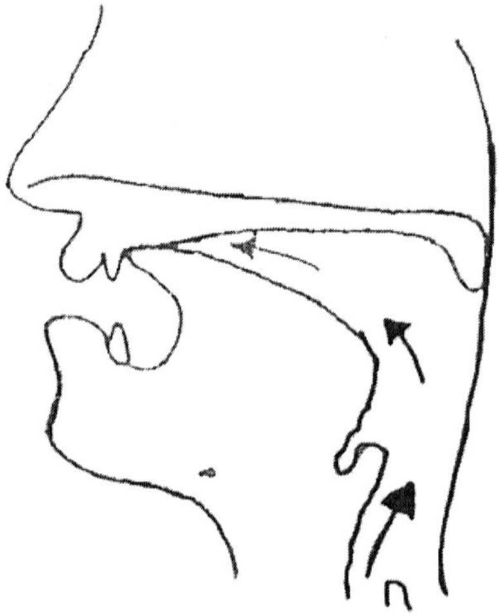

/t/ and /d/

Distribution

It occurs in all the three positions.

Spelling

In writing, it is realized by the letter 'd' as in 'dress' and 'dd' as in 'add'. The letter 'd' is also pronounced as /t/ when it is followed by /θ/ as in the word width.

/k/ as in kin, skin, trick, etc. For the articulations of this sound vocal cords are wide apart and so they do not vibrate. It is, therefore, a voiceless sound. The back of the tongue forms complete closure with the soft palate and this closure is ended abruptly resulting in the compressed air escaping with plosion. It is thus a voiceless velar plosive. It is a fortis sound.

Allophones

It has the following allophones.

(a) Aspirated [k] when in the stressed initial position as in 'kin', (b) unaspirated [p] when preceded by 's' and when in an unstressed syllable as in 'skin', (c) unexploded [k] when in the final position as in 'trick', (d) advanced [d] when followed by a front or central vowel as in 'keep', 'walker', etc., (e) retracted when followed by a back vowel as in 'school' and (f) lip rounded when followed by a rounded vowel as in 'school' and lip spread when followed by an unrounded vowel as in 'keep'.

Spelling

In writing, this sound is realized by the letter 'k' as in 'keep', 'c' as in 'cool', 'cc' as in 'occur', 'ck' as in 'trick', etc. This sound is not produced when the letter 'k' is followed by 'n' in spelling as in knee, know, knack, etc.

/g/ as in gut, luggage, big, etc. This sound is different from /k/ only in respect of the state of the glottis. For the production of this sound the vocal cords are loosely held together and so there is vibration. This is a voiced velar plosive. It is a lenis sound.

Allophones

It has the following allophones.

(a) Partially devoiced [g] when it occurs at the end of a word as in 'fig', (b) lip rounded when followed by a rounded vowel as in 'good', (c) lip spread when followed by an unrounded vowel as in 'geese', (d) advanced when followed by a front vowel as in 'geese', (e) retracted when followed by a back vowel as in 'goose' and (f) unexploded when in the final position as in 'big'.

Spelling

In writing, it is realized by the letter 'g' as in 'gum' and 'gg' as in 'luggage'. The letter 'g' is not pronounced when it is followed by the letter 'n' as in 'gnat' or by the letter 'm' as in 'phlegm'. But when a new word is formed by adding a suffix, it is pronounced. So in the word 'phlegmatic' it will be pronounced.

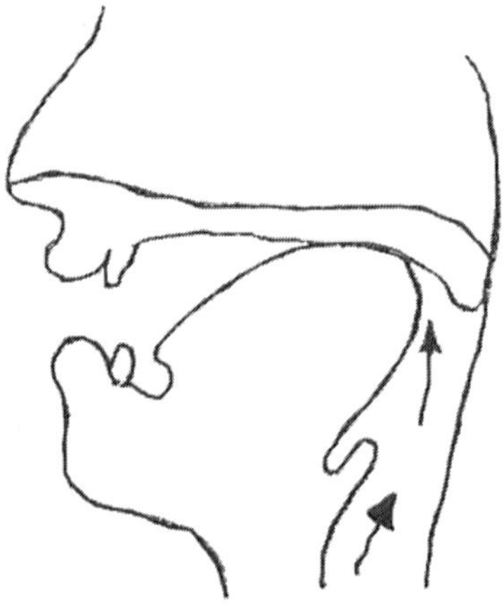

/k/ and /g/

5.2.2 Affricates

Affricates constitutes the next class of consonants. There are two affricates in English.

/tʃ/ as in chip, factual, preach, etc. For this sound the vocal cords are wide apart, so there is no vibration and the sound is voiceless. The tip of the tongue and the alveolar ridge come in close and firm contact and the front is raised toward the hard palate but instead of the contact getting removed suddenly as in the case of a plosive it is removed gradually and slowly and so the compressed air is released gradually. It is thus a voiceless palato-alveolar affricate.

Allophones

It has two allophones-lip rounded as in 'choose' and lip spread as in 'cheese'.

Distribution

It occurs in all three positions as in the examples above.

Spelling

In writing, it is realized by 'ch' as in 'chip', 'tch' as in 'match', 't+u' as in 'future', 't+ion' as in 'question', etc.

/dʒ/ as in jar, ajar, rage, etc. The difference between this consonant and the previous one is that for the articulation of this sound the vocal cords are loosely held together and so this is a voiced sound unlike the previous voiceless sound. In other respects, it is like the previous sound. It is, therefore, a voiced palato-alveolar affricate.

Allophones

It has three allophones—lip rounded as in 'juice', lip spread as in 'jeep' and devoiced as in 'rage'.

Distribution

It occurs in all three positions as in the examples above.

Spelling

In writing, it is realized by 'j' as in 'jar', 'g' as in 'orange', 'gg' as in 'suggest', 'dg' as in 'budget', 'di' as in 'soldier', etc.

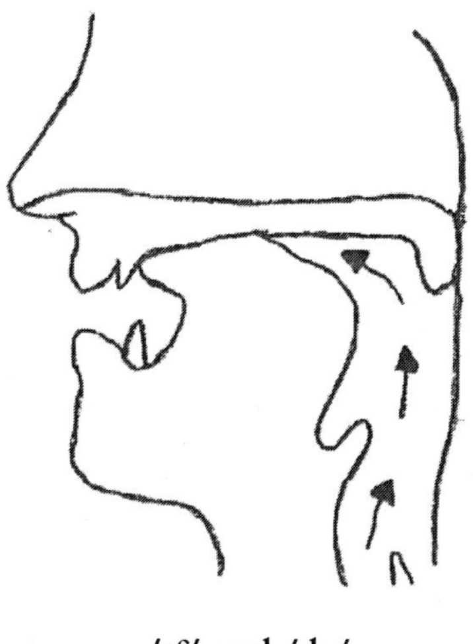

/tʃ/ and /dʒ/

5.2.3 Nasals

English has a set of three nasals.

For all of them the vocal cords are loosely held together and the soft palate is lowered. The difference lies only in the place of articulation.

/m/ as in main, admit, fame, etc. This nasal is produced when the lower lip and the upper lip come in close contact and the trapped air is not allowed to escape through the oral tract. It goes out through the nasal cavity as the soft palate is lowered. It is, thus, a voiced bilabial nasal.

Allophones

It has the following allophones.

(a) Devoiced [m] when preceded by a voiceless sound as in 'topmost', (b) labio-dental [m] when followed by a dental sound as in 'circumvent', (c) partially devoiced when it occurs finally as in 'name', (d) lip rounded when followed by a rounded vowel as in 'moon', (e) lip spread when followed by an unrounded vowel as in 'mean', etc.

Distribution

It occurs in all three positions as in the examples above.

Spelling

In writing, it is realized by the letter 'm' as in 'moon' and 'mm' as in 'summer'.

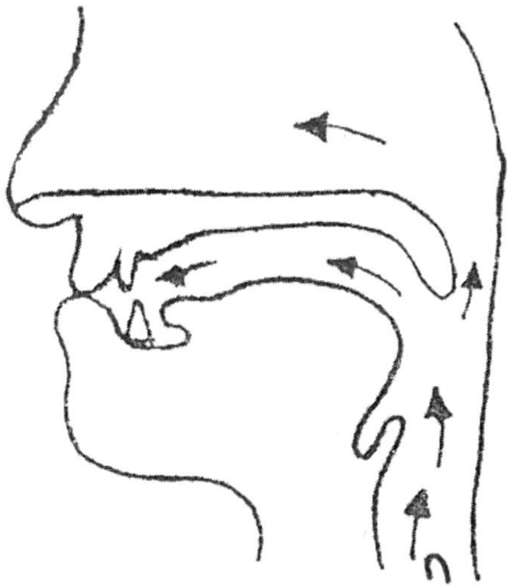

/m/

/n/ as in name, inmate, mane, etc. For this sound the tip of the tongue and the alveolar ridge are in firm contact, the blocked air once again escapes through the nasal cavity as the soft palate is lowered. It is a voiced alveolar nasal.

Allophones

It has the following allophones.

(a) Dental [n] when followed by a dental sound as in 'tenth', (b) partially devoiced [n] when preceded by a voiceless sound as in 'snug', (c) post-alveolar when followed by a post-alveolar sound as in 'henry', (d) syllabic when it performs the function of a vowel in a syllable as in 'button' where the word has two syllables—but/ton but in speech there is no vowel in the second syllable. In such a situation the final /n/ performs the function of a syllable and is known as syllabic [n], (e) lip rounded when followed by a lip rounded vowel as in 'noon' and (f) lip spread when followed by an unrounded vowel as in 'neat'.

Distribution

It occurs in all three positions as in the examples above.

Spelling

In writing, it is realized by 'n' as in 'name', 'nn' as in 'sinner'. The letter 'n' is not pronounced at the end of a word if it is preceded by the letter 'm' as in 'autumn', 'column', etc., but when a new word is formed by adding a suffix, it is pronounced. So in 'autumnal' it is pronounced.

/ŋ/ as in singer, sing, etc. For the articulation of this sound the back of the tongue comes in contact with the soft palate and the soft palate is lowered, so the blocked air escapes through the nasal cavity. It is, therefore, a voiced velar nasal.

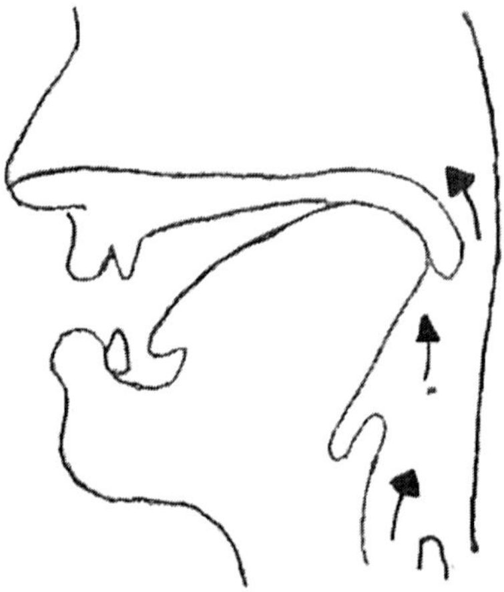

/ŋ/

Allophones

It has the following allophones.

(a) Advanced when preceded by a front vowel as in 'sing' and (b) retracted when preceded by a back vowel as in 'song'.

Distribution

Unlike the other nasals it does not occur in the initial position.

Spelling

In spelling, it is realized when the letter 'n' is followed by a velar plosive as in 'sink' and 'sing'.

5.2.4 Lateral

English has only one lateral sound.

/l/ as in lame, help, male, etc. For the articulation of this sound the vocal cords are loosely held together producing vibration and voice, the tip of the tongue and the teeth ridge come in close contact completely blocking the central passage of the air but either one side or both sides of the tongue are lowered to allow the air to escape through the lateral passage. It is thus a voiced alveolar lateral.

Allophones

It has the following allophones.

(a) Clear [l] when it occurs initially, before a vowel and before /j/ as in 'laugh', 'love', 'lure', etc., (b) dark [l] when it occurs before a consonant as in 'bulk' or finally as in 'ball'. For this allophone the back of the tongue is also raised simultaneously towards the soft palate or the velum and this sound is velarized, (c) syllabic [l] when it functions as a syllabic element as in 'bottle', (d) voiceless [l] when preceded by stressed /p/ and /k/ sounds as in 'play', 'clay', etc., (e) lip rounded when followed by a rounded vowel as in 'loose' and (f) lip spread when followed by an unrounded vowel as in 'lease'.

Distribution

It occurs in all three positions as in the examples above.

Spelling

In spelling, it is realized by 'l' as in 'lame' and 'll' as in 'fall'. The letter 'l' is not pronounced when it is followed by 'm' as in 'calm', 'balm', 'almond', etc. and when it is preceded by a long vowel and followed by another consonant as in 'walk', 'talk', etc.

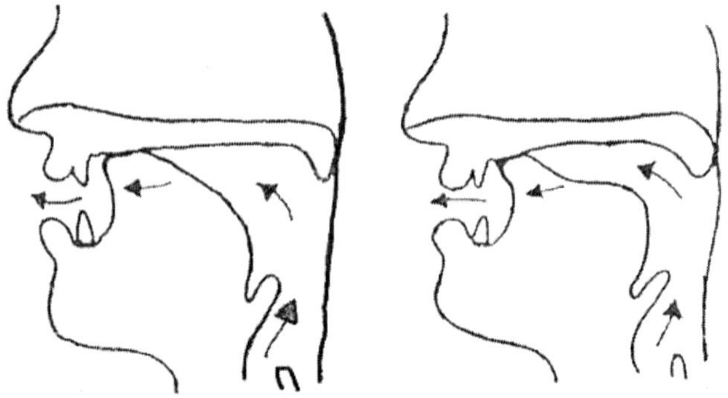

Clear [l] Dark [l]

5.2.5 Frictionless Continuant

English has one such sound.

/r/ as in red, arrive, etc. This consonant has been described in different ways. Daniel Jones calls it a fricative, A.C. Gimson a frictionless continuant and J.D. O'Connor a glide. For Ladefoged, it is an approximant. For the production of this sound the vocal cords are wide apart resulting in absence of vibration and voice, the tip of the tongue is raised towards the back of the alveolar ridge but there is no obstruction to the passage of air. So the air escapes freely without friction. It has, therefore, been described as a voiceless frictionless continuant. Although there is no narrowing or closure causing friction and the outgoing air escapes freely as in the case of a vowel, it is classified as a consonant because in a syllable it performs the function of a consonant.

Allophones

(a) /r/ becomes voiced fricative when it is preceded by a voiced sound as in 'gray', 'grow', 'dry', etc., (b) voiceless fricative when followed by accented /p/, /t/ and /k/ as in 'pray', 'tray', 'cry', etc., (c) partially devoiced when preceded by unaccented /p/, /t/ and /k/ as in 'spray', 'stray', 'screw', etc., (d) alveolar flap or tap [r] in inter-vocalic position or after /θ/ and /ð/ as in 'arrive' , 'three', 'with respect', etc. In fact, for this sound the organs of speech involved meet and part several times and this manner is therefore called 'intermittent closure', (e) lip rounded when followed by a rounded vowel as in 'room' and (f) lip spread when followed by an unrounded vowel as in 'ream'.

Distribution

It occurs initially and medially as in the examples above.

Spelling

In spelling, it is realized by the letter 'r' and 'rr' as in 'range', 'arrange', etc. The letter 'r' is not pronounced when it occurs in post-vocalic and final positions as in 'farm' and 'far'. It is pronounced in pre-vocalic and initial positions as in 'tray' and 'dry'. However, there are two types of English-speaking people, the 'r' pronouncing or 'rhotic' and the non-'r' pronouncing or the 'non-rhotic'. R.P. speakers belong to the second type. But let us look at the following.

Linking /r/: We have seen that R.P. speakers do not pronounce the letter 'r' when it occurs finally. However, when a word ends in the letter 'r' and the following word begins with a vowel, R.P. speakers pronounce the letter 'r' as in 'far and near'. Here the 'r' of 'far' will be pronounced because it is followed by a vowel but the 'r' of 'near' will not be pronounced because it occurs finally and there is no sound after this. This variety of /r/ is called linking /r/.

Intrusive /r/: R.P. speakers also pronounce the /r/ sound even when the letter 'r' is not present in spelling. This is done when a word ends in a vowel and the following word also begins with a vowel as in 'The sofa is good'. An R.P. speaker will speak this sentence as 'The sofar is good'. This is called intrusive /r/. This variety is also used in American English. This, however, has come in for criticism by many B.B.C. listeners. Nevertheless, it is used widely.

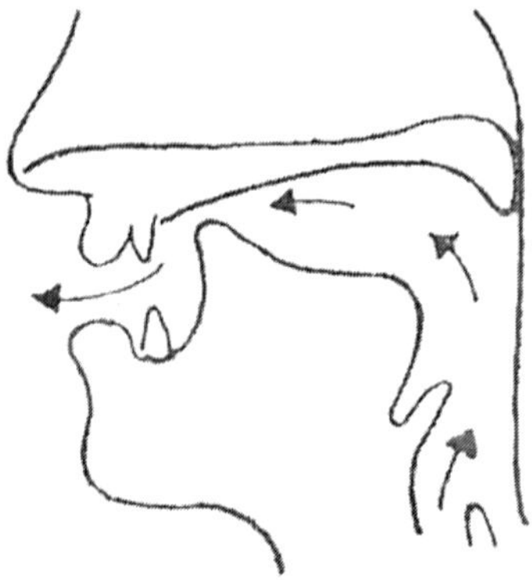

/r/

5.2.6 Fricatives

English has nine fricatives.

/f/ as in fur, suffer, cough, etc. For the articulation of this consonant the vocal cords are wide apart resulting in absence of vibration and voice, the lower lip comes close to the upper row of teeth and so there is narrowing of the air passage. It is thus a voiceless labio-dental fricative.

Allophones

It has two allophones, lip rounded when followed by rounded vowel as in 'boot' and lip spread when followed by an unrounded vowel as in 'beat'.

Distribution

It occurs in all three positions as in the examples above.

Spelling

In writing, it is realized by 'f' as in 'far', 'ff' as in 'off', 'ph' as in 'photo', 'gh' as in 'rough', etc.

/v/ as in vase, saver, above, etc. For the articulation of this sound the vocal cords are loosely held together and so this is a voiced sound. The place and manner of articulation are the same as for /f/. It is, therefore, a voiced labio-dental fricative.

Allophones

Besides the lip rounded and lip spread allophones it has a devoiced variety when it occurs finally.

Distribution

It occurs in all three positions as in the examples above.

Spelling

In writing, it is realized by 'v' as in 'save', 'vv' as in 'savvy', 'f' as in 'of', 'ph' as in 'nephew', etc.

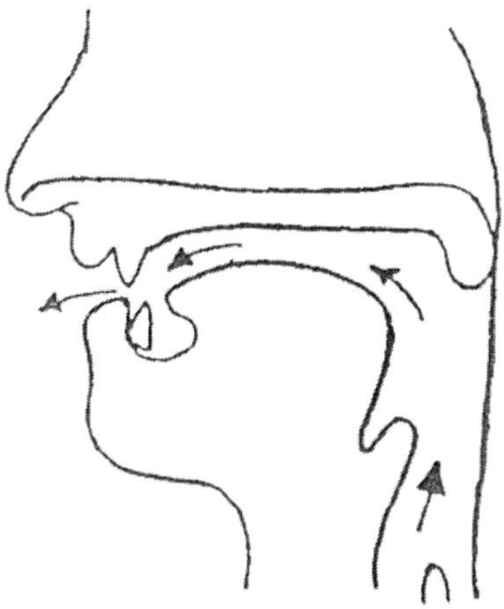

/f/ and /v/

/θ/ as in thick, something, wealth, etc. For this sound the vocal cords are wide apart resulting in absence of vibration and voice, the tip of the tongue and the rim brush lightly against the back of the upper incisors and there is narrowing of the vocal tract. So it is a voiceless dental fricative. It is also called inter-dental because the tip of the tongue may protrude between the two rows of teeth.

Allophones

It has lip rounded and lip spread allophones as in 'thought' and 'theme'.

Distribution

It occurs in all three positions as in the examples above.

/ð/ as in this, mother, with, etc. For the articulation of this sound the vocal cords are loosely held together producing vibration and voice. In other respects, it is like /θ/. It is therefore a voiced dental fricative.

Allophones

Besides the lip rounded and lip spread varieties it has a devoiced allophone when it is in the final position.

Distribution

It occurs in all three positions as in the examples above.

Spelling

In spelling, it is realized by 'th' as in 'this'.

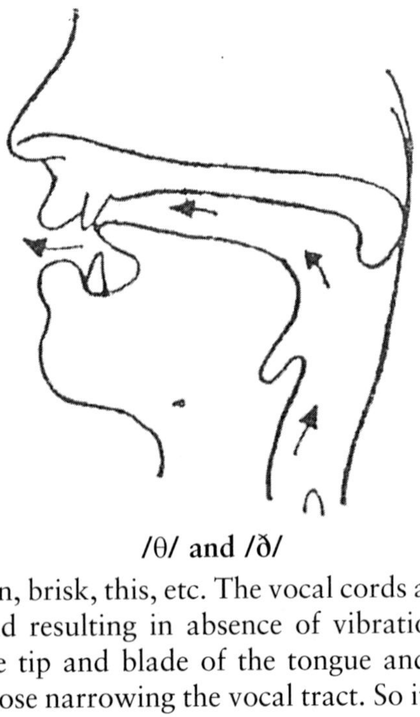

/θ/ and /ð/

/s/ as in sin, brisk, this, etc. The vocal cords are wide apart for this sound resulting in absence of vibration and voice, the tip or the tip and blade of the tongue and the alveolar ridge come close narrowing the vocal tract. So it is a voiceless alveolar fricative.

Allophones

It has lip rounded and lip spread varieties as in 'soon' and 'scene', respectively.

Distribution

It occurs in all three positions as in the examples above.

Spelling

In writing, it is realized by 's' as in 'soon', 'ss' as in 'hiss', 'c' as in 'face', 'sc' as in 'science', 'z' as in 'pretzel', 'zz' as in 'pizza', 'x' as in 'exit', etc. The letter 'x' represents two sounds. If the first sound is /k/, the second sound will be /s/.

/z/ as in zoom, drizzle, lose, etc. For this sound the vocal cords are held loosely together, so there is vibration and voice. In other respects it is like /s/. It is thus a voiced alveolar fricative.

Allophones

Besides the lip rounded and lip spread varieties it has a devoiced allophone when it occurs finally as in 'lose'.

Distribution

It occurs in all three positions as in the examples above.

Spelling

In writing, it is realized by 's' as in 'his' and 'clubs' (In plural nouns 's' is pronounced as /z/ when the singular form ends in a voiced sound except /d/ and /z/.), 'ss' as in 'scissors', 'z' as in 'zebra', 'zz' as in 'jazz', 'x' when the first sound is /g/, etc.

/ʃ/ as in shop, social, dish, etc. For the articulation of this sound the vocal cords are wide apart resulting in absence of vibration and voice, the tip and blade of the tongue come close to the teeth ridge and the front of the tongue is raised towards the hard palate causing narrowing of the vocal tract. So it is a voiceless palato-alveolar fricative.

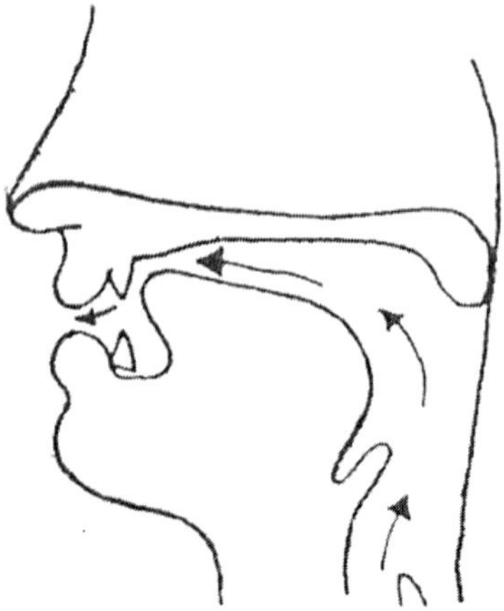

/s/ and /z/

Allophones

It has lip rounded and lip spread varieties as in shoe and she.

Distribution

It occurs in all three positions as in the examples above.

Spelling

In writing, it is realized by 's' as in 'sure', 'ss' as in 'assure', 'sh' as in 'shoe', 'ch' as in 'chauffeur', 'ce' as in 'ocean', 'sci' as in 'conscience', 'ci' as in 'special', 'x' as in 'luxury' but not in 'luxurious' or 'luxuriant'.

/ʒ / as in genre, measure, garage, etc. For the articulation of this sound the vocal cords are held loosely together producing vibration and voice. In other respects it is like /ʃ/. It is, therefore, a voiced palato-alveolar fricative.

Allophones

It does not have a lip rounded variety. It has a devoiced variety in the final position.

Distribution

It occurs in all three positions but the frequency is very low in the initial and final positions.

Spelling

In writing, this is realized by 'si' as in 'decision', 'su' as in 'pleasure', 'ge' as in 'garage', 'zu' as in 'azure', etc.

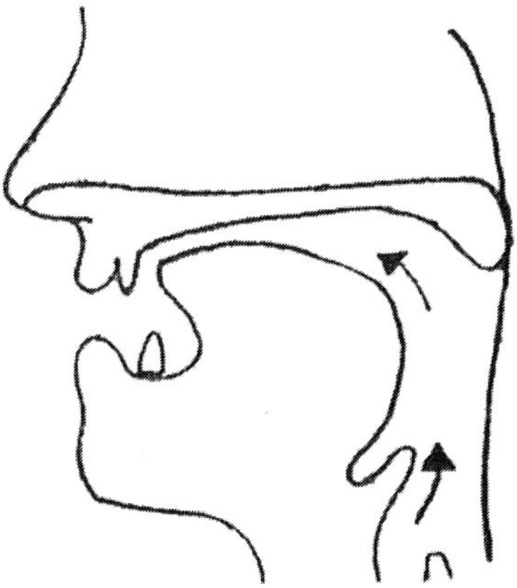

/ʃ/ and /ʒ/

/h/ as in hope, behind, etc. For the articulation of this sound the vocal cords are held wide apart, resulting in absence of vibration and voice and there is narrowing at the glottis. It is, therefore, a voiceless glottal fricative. It is regarded as simply the voiceless counterpart of the following vowel sound.

Allophones

It has the following allophones.

(a) Voiced /h/ in intervocalic position as in 'behind', (b) lip rounded as in 'whom', and (c) lip spread as in 'heat'.

Distribution

It occurs in syllable initial pre-vocalic position only as in the examples above. It can occur only before vowels or /j/. It can also occur before /w/ when this sound becomes voiceless.

Spelling

In writing, it is realized by the letter 'h'. It is not pronounced when it is preceded by 'w' as in 'whistle', etc. but in 'who' and 'whom' it is 'w' which is not pronounced and 'h' is pronounced.

5.2.7 Semi-vowel

A semi-vowel shares the formal properties of a vowel but in respect of function it is like a consonant. It is said to be "a rapid vocalic glide on to a syllabic sound of a greater steady duration". Because it performs the function of a consonant, so it is included among consonants. There are two semi-vowels in English.

/w/ as in war, quick, etc. For this sound the vocal cords are held loosely together and produce vibration and voice, the lips are rounded and at the same time the back of the tongue is raised towards the soft palate but there is no obstruction or narrowing of the air passage. It is, therefore, a voiced bilabial semi-vowel. It is also described as voiced labio-velar semi-vowel because of the fact that there is co-articulation of the back of the tongue and the soft palate.

Allophones

This consonant becomes devoiced when it is preceded by /t/ and /k/ in a stressed syllable as in 'twin', 'quick', etc. and when the letter 'w' is followed by 'h' in spelling as in 'what', 'where', etc. Gimson, however, calls it a fricative and not a semi-vowel when it gets devoiced because of this.

Distribution

It occurs only initially and medially.

Spelling

In writing, it is realized by 'w' as in 'war', 'wh' as in 'what', 'o' as in 'one', 'oi' as in 'choir', 'ui' as in 'suite', 'ua' as in 'quality', 'qu' as in 'quick'. The letter 'w' is not pronounced when it is followed by 'r' as in 'write', 'wry', etc. and by 'h' as in 'who'. In other words, beginning with 'w' and followed by 'h', 'w' is pronounced and 'h' remains silent as in 'when', 'why', etc.

/j/ as in yet, tube, etc. For this sound also the vocal cords are held loosely together producing vibration and voice, the front of the tongue is raised towards the hard palate but there is no obstruction or narrowing and the air escapes freely as for a vowel. The lips are unrounded. So this is an unrounded palatal semi-vowel.

Allophones

It gets devoiced when it is preceded by /p/, /t/ and /k/ in a stressed syllable as in 'pure', 'tune', 'queue', etc.

Distribution

It occurs initially and medially.

Spelling

In writing, it is realized by 'y' as in 'yes', 'u' as in 'tune', 'eau' as in 'beauty', 'ew' as in 'few', 'iew' as in 'view' and 'ue' as in 'queue', etc.

/r/, /l/, /w/ and /j/ are described as approximant by Ladefoged. He describes /r/, /w/ and /j/ as central approximants and /l/ as lateral approximant. They become largely voiceless when they are preceded by voiceless stops.

Note: The section on spelling, it has to be noted, is not exhaustive. English has borrowed heavily from different languages and this process is still continuing. Many words are being borrowed from a host of languages. So we can find other possibilities in the language.

This chart of English consonants shows three labels for each sound.

Consonants of English (R.P.)

		Manner of articulation											
		Plosive		Affricate		Nasal		Fricative		Lateral		Approximants	
		vl	vd	vl	vd	vl	vd	vl	vd	vl	vd	vl	vd
Place of articulation	Bilabial	p	b				m						W
	Labio – dental							f	v				
	Dental							θ	ð				
	Alveolar	t	d				n	s	z		l		
	Post – alveolar												r
	Palato - alveolar			tʃ	dʒ			ʃ	ʒ				
	Palatal												j
	Velar	K	g				ŋ						
	Glottal							h					
	vl– voiceless vd – voiced												

5.2.8 Consonants in the Speech of Indian Speakers

5.2.8.1 *Plosives*: (a) Indian speakers of English do not generally aspirate the voiceless plosives /p/, /t/ and /k/ in the stressed initial position as is done by the native speakers. So 'pin' is pronounced as [pin] and not as [phin], 'tin' as [tin] and not as [thin] and 'card' as [kard] and not as [kha:d]. This can cause loss of intelligibility for native speakers as they may hear these words as 'bin', 'din' and 'guard', respectively. If someone says 'The child has swallowed a pin' without aspirating the 'p' of 'pin', it may be heard as 'The child has swallowed a bin'. This will be an amazing feat for the listener and he may be tempted to refer it to the *Guinness Book of World Records*. Similarly, 'pray' without aspirated 'p' may be heard as 'bray'.

(b) Indian speakers aspirate /b/, /d/ and /g/ when in spelling the letters 'b', 'd' and 'g' are followed by the letter 'h'. So they aspirate /b/, /d/ and /g/ in words like 'abhor', 'adhere' and 'ghost'.

(c) /t/ and /d/ are not articulated as alveolar plosives but as retroflex sounds. This may result in loss of communication when interacting with a native speaker.

(d) The final /t/ and /d/ sounds are dropped in words like 'best', 'dressed', 'robbed', etc.

5.2.8.2 *Affricates*: If two affricate sounds occur in a sequence the first one is not released as in 'watch chain', 'orange juice', etc.

5.2.8.3 *Nasals*: While Indian speakers have no difficulty in pronouncing /m/ and /n/ correctly they tend to pronounce the letter 'g' after the nasal sound /ŋ/ as in 'sing', 'thing', etc. pronouncing them as /siŋg/ and /thiŋg/ and not as /siŋ/ and /thiŋ/ as native speakers do.

5.2.8.4 *Lateral*: (a) Indian speakers by and large tend to disregard the distinction between the clear and the dark varieties of the lateral /l/ and use the former in all the positions. (b) They do not also use the syllabic /l/ and introduce a vowel sound, either /i/ or /ə/, between the final lateral sound and the preceding sound. Thus 'mettle' is pronounced as 'metel', 'meddle' as 'medel' and 'middle' as 'midil'.

5.2.8.5 *Frictionless Continuant*: Indians belong to the rhotic or 'r' pronouncing group and so they pronounce /r/ whenever there is the letter 'r' in spelling. However, linking /r/ and intrusive /r/ are not found in the speech of Indian speakers.

5.2.8.6 *Fricatives*: Indian speakers do not always pronounce these sounds as the R.P. speakers do.

(a) /f/ and /v/ are not pronounced as labio-dental fricatives but as bilabial fricatives. Some speakers articulate them as bilabial aspirated plosives. This results in loss of meaning in pairs like pair-fair, peal-feel, pine-fine, etc. because the native speaker pronounces the first words of the pairs with the aspirated variety of the phoneme /p/ and the Indian speaker pronounces the second word with this allophone of the /p/ phoneme. There is also the tendency to add the sound /h/ to /v/ making it /vh/. Also, /v/ and /w/ are articulated in the same way, thus doing away with the minimal pair distinction between 'vest' and 'west'.

(b) /θ/ and /ð/ Indian speakers usually pronounce these fricatives as aspirated dental plosives. Indian speakers also find difficulty in articulating these sounds when they are followed by /s/ and /z/ and tend to drop them. Thus words like 'months' and 'clothes' are pronounced without the fricative sounds.

(c) /s/ and /z/ Some Indian speakers produce these sounds in such a manner that meaning is confused; they replace /s/ by /ʃ/ and /ʃ/ by /s/. Thus 'sip' and 'ship', 'save' and 'shave', 'seat' and 'sheet', etc. lose their minimal pair distinction. Another problem with Indian speakers is that they generally introduce a vowel, /i/ or /ə/ before or after the /s/ sound. Thus 'school' becomes 'ischool' or 'sechool' and 'spring' becomes 'ispring' or 'sepring'. Again distinction between /s/ and /z/ is not maintained in the plural and possessive endings of nouns and third person singular verbs in the present form. So the letter 's' in words like 'docks' and 'dogs' is pronounced in the same way causing confusion to the native speaker. Some speakers replace /z/ by either /s/ or /dʒ/. This results in loss of minimal pair distinction between words like 'buzz' and 'budge' or 'buzz' and 'bus', 'falls' and 'false', etc.

(d) The problem with /ʃ/ is the same as for /s/. /ʒ/ is replaced by most speakers with /z/, so 'meaʒure' becomes [mezə]. Some speakers replace it with /dʒ/.

(e) /h/ It does not cause any problem to the Indian speakers but they tend to pronounce the /h/ sound when the letter 'h' occurs after 'w' in writing in words like 'what', 'white', 'where', etc.

5.2.8.7 *Semi-vowels*: (a) /w/ Indian speakers tend to replace /w/ with a bilabial fricative. Also the distinction between /v/ and /w/ is not maintained. So the minimal pair distinction between words like 'worse' and 'verse' is lost.

(b) /j/ Indian speakers tend to drop it in the initial position and pronounce words like 'year' /jɪə/ and 'ear' /ɪə/ in the same way. This leads to an error in the use of the indefinite article 'a/an'.

Exercise

1. Describe the front vowels of English (R.P.) with appropriate examples.
2. Draw a vowel diagram and place the pure vowels on it.
3. Describe the centring diphthongs of English (R.P.) and give at least two examples of each.
4. Describe the plosive consonants of English (R.P.) mentioning their allophones.
5. Write short notes on the following:
   (a) Clear 'l'
   (b) Dark 'l'
   (c) Linking 'r'
   (d) Intrusive 'r'
6. How does Daniel Jones' description of pure vowels and diphthongs of English (R.P.) differ from that of A.C. Gimson?
7. Why do the symbols assigned by Gimson and Jones for the nearly half-close front unrounded vowel differ?
8. Give three-term labels for the following phonemes of English (R.P.).
   (a) /p/
   (b) /m/
   (c) /j/

(d) /w/
(e) /k/
(f) /z/
(g) /e/
(h) /i:/
(i) /r/
(j) /f/

9. Give the I.P.A. symbols for the following:
   (a) voiceless dental fricative
   (b) voiced palate-alveolar fricative
   (c) voiced velar nasal
   (d) voiceless glottal fricative
   (e) front nearly half-close unrounded vowel
   (f) back nearly close rounded vowel
   (g) half-open central unrounded vowel
   (h) between half-open and half-close front unrounded vowel
   (i) voiced bilabial plosive
   (j) voiced alveolar nasal

10. Complete the following statements by selecting the correct alternative given below each statement.
    (a) English (R.P.) has
        (i) twenty-four phonemes
        (ii) forty-four phonemes
        (iii) twelve phonemes
        (iv) twenty phonemes
    (b) There are .... states of the glottis.
        (i) three
        (ii) two
        (iii) four
        (iv) five

(c) There are .... pure front vowels in English (R.P.).
   (i) two
   (ii) six
   (iii) four
   (iv) five

(d) Fricatives differ from the plosives in
   (i) the manner of articulation
   (ii) place of articulation
   (iii) state of the glottis
   (iv) position of the soft palate

(e) Plosives and affricates are different from each other in the
   (i) closure stage of articulation
   (ii) hold stage of the articulation
   (iii) the above two stages of articulation
   (iv) release stage of articulation

(f) A nasal sound is produced when the soft palate is
   (i) raised
   (ii) lowered
   (iii) partly raised
   (iv) slightly raised

(g) English (R.P.) has ...... aspirated consonant phoneme.
   (i) one
   (ii) four
   (iii) no
   (iv) two

11. Find out the phonemes of your mother tongue and give their I.P.A. symbols.

6

Syllable

6.1 Introduction

A word is constituted either of a single sound like 'ɪ' or 'oh' or a string of sounds like 'war', 'water', etc. When we speak the first three words we produce all the sounds together but when we produce the word 'water', we have to break it into two parts, 'wa' and 'ter'. The part of the word that is spoken together is known as a syllable. So 'ɪ', 'oh' and 'war' are words and at the same time syllables. A syllable, therefore, may constitute a full word or part of a word. It is, therefore, different from a word. A syllable is also different from a morpheme. The word 'beginner' has three syllables but only two morphemes. The word 'worker' has two syllables and also two morphemes. So a syllable may or may not be a morpheme. (A morpheme is the smallest meaningful unit in the grammatical system of a language.) In 'beginner' we have the meaningful units 'begin' and 'er'. Similarly in 'worker' we have two meaningful units 'work' and 'er'.

According to Peter Roach, a syllable can be defined both phonetically and phonologically, that is, the way it is pronounced and the way it functions in a language. It consists of a centre, a sound in the production of which there is no obstruction to the flow of the outgoing air, which is a vowel. This sound is comparatively loud. It can be preceded and followed by sounds for which there is some kind of obstruction or narrowing of the air passage, that is, a consonant. So a syllable is made of a vowel which functions as the centre and is the obligatory element and consonants which are marginal or peripheral elements and are optional.

For David Abercrombie "a syllable is a movement, mostly an audible movement". This means that in speaking a syllable we move from one sound to the other which can be heard.

A.C. Gimson defines a syllable on the basis of two theories, namely, the prominence theory and the pulse theory.

6.1.1 The Prominence Theory

According to this theory when we utter a word, some sounds appear to be more prominent than the others. It is these sounds which determine the number of syllables in a word. They are known as peaks of prominence. The sounds which constitute the peak of prominence are louder. This is acoustic and based on the auditory judgement. These prominent sounds are usually vowels. In the word 'war' there is only one vowel and therefore only one syllable. But 'water' has two peaks of prominence in 'wa', and 'ter', the second sound in these chunks of the utterance. So it has two syllables. It is the relative sonority of the sounds that constitute the utterance which determines the number of syllables. Prominence is formed by this sonority combined with length, stress and pitch.

6.1.2 The Pulse Theory

The speech act is a muscular activity. Because of this muscular activity speech sounds are produced. When this activity takes place we produce puffs of air which are responsible for producing a group of sounds. One puff of air is produced by one chest-pulse, a contraction of the muscles of the rib cage that pushes more air out of the lungs, and only one sound or one group of sounds can be produced by it. So the pulse or the chest-pulse produces a sound or a string of sounds. This constitutes a syllable. In 'war' all the sounds are produced by one chest-pulse, so it has only one syllable. But we need two chest-pulses to produce all the sounds of 'water'.

One chest-pulse produces 'wa' and the other 'ter'. So 'water' has two syllables. Chest-pulse is also known as breath-pulse and syllable-pulse. It is the vowel that carries the chest-pulse. Thus the number of syllables in an utterance will depend on the number of vowels in it. This theory put forward by R.H. Stetson is based on physiological principle. But sometimes double chest-pulse cannot be observed as in 'seeing'. So it can be linguistically misleading.

Peter Ladefoged, however, says that there is no agreed definition of a syllable. According to him "syllables are best defined in terms of the activities of the speaker". They can be defined "in terms of some measurable combination of respiratory and pharyngeal activity". He also observes that "syllables may be considered to be abstract units that exist at some higher level in the mental activity of the speaker". Ladefoged finds both the above theories unsatisfactory because they do not truly state what a syllable is. As regards the first theory, he thinks that it is not possible to think of a procedure for combining sonority, length, stress and pitch so as to form prominence. As regards the chest-pulse theory, he observes that "direct investigations of the activities of the muscles have failed to confirm this theory".

6.2 Structure of a Syllable

A syllable is made of three parts. They are (a) onset or releasing, (b) closure or arresting or coda and (c) nucleus or core. The word 'pin' has one peak of prominence and can be spoken with one chest pulse and one puff of air. So it consists of only one syllable. It has three parts—/p/, /ɪ/ and /n/. The first part, that is /p/, is the onset while the last part /n/ is the closure element or coda. The vowel /ɪ/ is the nucleus. It is not possible to have a syllable without a nucleus because it constitutes the peak of prominence and carries the chest-pulse. This nucleus is usually a vowel. Let us look at another word. 'I' is a full word and a syllable in English but it has only a vowel and no marginal elements, that is, consonants. So it has neither the onset nor the closure. The onset and closure are consonants. Here we do not have either the onset or the arresting element. If there are no onset and closure we have zero onset and zero closure. In a syllable the onset can be designated as C1, the nucleus as V and the closure as C2. A syllable can thus have the structure of the following types:

(a) V—nucleus only as in 'ɪ',

(b) C1V—onset or releasing consonant and nucleus as in 'we',

(c) VC2—nucleus and arresting consonant as in 'it' and

(d) C1VC2—releasing consonant or onset, nucleus and arresting consonant or closure as in 'bit'.

The syllable structure can also be expressed in the following way (C1) V (C2). The brackets indicate that the elements inside are optional while absence of brackets indicates that the element is obligatory.

In a syllable there can be one or more consonants in the releasing and arresting positions but there cannot be more than one vowel or nucleus. For example, in the word 'ray' there is only one releasing element but in 'tray' there are two and in 'stray' there are three. Similarly in 'led' there is only one arresting consonant but in 'lend' there are two and in 'lends' there are three. Sometimes a consonant may perform the function of nucleus instead of a vowel as we saw in the previous chapter. In the English word 'little' which has two syllables, 'lit/tle', the second syllable is without a vowel but it does have a nucleus. Here in the second syllable /l/ functions as the nucleus. We have seen that consonants which perform the function of a vowel in a syllable are called syllabic consonants.

A word can consist of one, two or more syllables. Words with only one syllable are called monosyllabic words, those with two syllables are called disyllabic words and those with more than two syllables are called polysyllabic words.

6.3 Types of Syllables

There can be two types of syllables depending upon the presence or absence of the closing or arresting element. They are (a) closed syllables containing at least one arresting element such as 'it', 'bit', etc. and (b) open syllables which do not contain a closing element such as 'way', 'say', etc.

6.4 Syllable Division

How to divide a disyllabic or a polysyllabic word into its component syllables is a problem and not always an easy task. For example, 'extra' has two syllables but how exactly they can be separated is difficult to decide. We have the following possibilities (a) ek/strə, (b) e/kstrə, (c) eks/trə, (d) ekst/rə and (e) ekstr/ə. However, most disyllabic or polysyllabic words can be divided into their component syllables without much difficulty.

If double letters occur in spelling they are apportioned to two different syllables. For example, 'button' will be divided into its components syllables as 'but/ton'. We put a bar between the two consonants to assign them to two different syllables.

6.5 Consonant Cluster and Abutting Consonants

We have seen that one, two or more consonants can occur in a syllable in either of the two positions. Consonants occurring in a sequence within a syllable are called consonant clusters as in the examples in 6.2. If, however, there is a sequence of consonants but they occur in two succeeding syllables they are known as abutting consonants as in the word 'mistake'. Though /s/ and /t/ occur in a sequence they do not belong to the same syllable. So they are abutting consonants.

6.6 Syllable Structure in English

The syllable structure in English can be expressed as (C0-3) V(C0-4). This means that in the releasing position there can be no or zero consonant or up to three consonants and in the closing position there can be either no or zero consonant or up to a maximum of four consonants. The following chart will exemplify it.

(i) I—no releasing and arresting consonant
(ii) Ray—one releasing consonant but no arresting consonant
(iii) Tray—two releasing consonants but no arresting consonant
(iv) Bled—two releasing consonants and one closing consonant
(v) Blend—two releasing consonants and two arresting consonants
(vi) Blends—two releasing consonants and three arresting consonants
(vii) Glimpsed—two releasing consonants and four arresting consonants
(viii) Stray—three releasing consonants but no arresting consonant
(ix) Stroke—three releasing consonants and one arresting consonant
(x) Stroked—three releasing consonants and two arresting consonants
(xi) Sick—one releasing consonant and one arresting consonant
(xii) Six—one releasing consonant and two arresting consonants
(xiii) Sixth—one releasing consonant and three arresting consonants
(xiv) Sixths—one releasing consonant and four arresting consonants
(xv) It—no releasing consonant and one arresting consonant
(xvi) Its—no releasing consonant and two arresting consonants
(xvii) Isn't—no releasing consonant and three arresting consonants.

It will appear from the above that English can have a consonant cluster of up to three consonants in the releasing position and a consonant cluster of up to four consonants in the arresting position.

Exercise

1. Define syllable and give suitable examples.
2. Discuss the prominence theory and pulse theory of syllable.
3. Why does Ladefoged think that both prominence theory and pulse theory fail to define a syllable?
4. Write a note on consonant cluster and abutting consonants and give examples from English.
5. Discuss the structure of syllable and give examples from English and your mother tongue.
6. Write a note on syllable structure of your mother tongue and give suitable examples.
7. Say whether the following statements are true or false.
   (a) Consonants are optional elements in a syllable.
   True False
   (b) The items inside the brackets are obligatory.
   True False
   (c) A syllable is different from a morpheme.
   True False
   (d) A syllable in English can have a maximum of two consonants before the vowel.
   True False
   (e) Coda is the releasing element in a syllable.
   True False
   (f) There can be a syllable without a vowel.
   True False
   (g) Syllables are of two types—open and close.
   True False
   (h) Abutting consonants belong to the same syllable.
   True False

7

Supra-segmental Features

Language, in order to be meaningful, has to be a chain. This is known as the syntagmatic relationship in language. The other relationship that is necessary for the language to perform satisfactorily is known as paradigmatic relationship or choice relationship where we have the option to choose an item in preference to other available items. The chain is formed by the segments, that is, vowels and consonants which form syllables and words. These are the segmental features of language. However, there are some other features which, though not responsible for forming the chain, play a very significant role in the communication of meaning. Incorrect use of these features often leads to faulty communication and loss of meaning. These features are known as supra-segmental features. Stress or accent is one such feature. Although in some cases stress and accent are used interchangeably, we shall do well to remember that accent is used to indicate a way of speaking such as American, British or Indian. It is also used to indicate some peculiarity in a person's speech. We may say that a particular person speaks with an accent. Accent has indexical function. Let us now look at what stress is and how it helps in communication of meaning.

7.1 What is Stress?

We have seen in Chapter 6 that when we speak we release puffs of air producing groups of sounds known as syllable which go to form words. Each syllable has a peak of prominence. In our speech every syllable that is spoken does not receive equal prominence. Some puffs of air may be stronger than the others. The word 'stronger' is spoken with two puffs of air producing two syllables, 'strong' and 'er' but the puff of air that produces the first syllable is stronger than the puff which produces the second syllable. As a result this first syllable becomes more prominent than the second one. Obviously greater degree of force has been applied in speaking the first syllable.

According to Daniel Jones, it is 'this degree of force with which a syllable is uttered' which we call stress. It involves a strong 'push' from the chest wall and therefore a strong force of exhalation and gives the impression of 'loudness'. According to A.C. Gimson, stress is 'relatively greater breath force or effort and muscular energy' applied to a syllable. It is the vowel-the central element or nucleus in a syllable—which receives the force and therefore the length of the vowel increases. Applying greater force also results in greater vibration of voiced sounds. The syllable which receives greater degree of force is known as stressed syllable and the one(s) which receives less force is/are called unstressed syllable(s). The stressed syllable is marked by putting a small vertical bar above and before that syllable while unstressed syllable(s) is/are left unmarked. Thus 'stronger' will be shown as ˈstronger indicating that it is the first syllable 'strong' which is stressed. This stressed syllable is heard more distinctly than the unstressed ones. In some cases both syllables of a disyllabic word may receive equal force and therefore both will be stressed, for example, 'ˈunˈdo', 'ˈfifˈteen', etc.

On the basis of the above it can be said that stressed syllables are louder than the unstressed ones, there is a pitch change, the length of the vowel makes it prominent and the vowel quality marks the stressed syllable.

According to Ladefoged, "stress can always be defined in terms of something a speaker does in one part of an utterance relative to another". He also believes that a stressed syllable is often, but not always, louder than an unstressed syllable. It is usually, but not always, on a higher pitch. The most reliable thing for a listener to detect is that a stressed syllable frequently has a longer vowel. A stressed syllable is usually accompanied by a rise in the pitch which is caused by an increase in the flow of air out of the lungs even without an increase in the activity of the laryngeal muscles.

7.2 Types of Stress

In polysyllabic words one of the syllables receives the greatest amount of force while one more syllable also receives force but not as much as the other one. The syllable which receives the maximum force is said to have primary stress and the one which receives more force than the rest but not as much as the syllable receiving primary stress is said to have secondary stress. Words like 'introduction', 'introspect', 'examination', etc., which are polysyllabic are pronounced in such a way that one of the syllables receives primary stress and one more syllable receives secondary stress. Secondary stress is indicated by putting a vertical bar below and before the syllable which receives the secondary stress. Thus stress pattern in the above words will be shown as follows: intros/pect, ˈintro/duction, and exami/nation.

7.3 Functions of Stress

Ladefoged also points out that stress can have three functions. (a) Emphasis or contrast as in the following example: 'John or Mary should go' and 'John and Mary should go'. In the first sentence 'John', 'Mary' and 'go' are stressed but in the second 'and' is also stressed and this brings out the emphasis which the speaker intends to give to the fact that both John and Mary are required to go and not only one of them.

(b) Stress also indicates the syntactic relationship between two word classes and their syntactic function. The noun-verb relationship can be indicated by placing the stress on two different syllables in words which have identical spelling but belong to different classes and perform two different functions in a syntactic structure. Thus 'insult' with stress on the first syllable will belong to the noun class and require the indefinite article 'an' and with stress on the second syllable belong to the verb class and cannot be preceded by 'an'; it can be preceded by 'to'.

(c) Stress also distinguishes a compound noun and an adjective followed by a noun that is an adjectival phrase, as in the phrase 'hot dog'. Compound nouns have a single stress on the first element, and a construction of an adjective followed by a noun has stress on both elements.

7.4 Stress in English

Stress in English is fixed as well as free. This means that once stress falls on a particular syllable in a word it will always fall on the same syllable unless a new word is formed from this word. For example, the word 'intoxicate' has stress on the second syllable but when a new word 'intoxication' is formed from this word which is a noun the primary stress shifts from the first syllable to the second last syllable, that is 'ca' and the syllable which received the stress in the verb form now receives secondary stress. Some other examples of such shift of stress are: aˈcademy-acaˈdemic-acadeˈmician, ˈpolitics-poˈlitical-poliˈtician, etc.

Stress is free in English because unlike in some other languages it does not fall on any fixed syllable in all the words. The position of stress varies. It may fall on the first syllable in a word but in another word it may fall on the second or the third syllable or on any other syllable. This means that in English word stress has to be learned separately for different words. One of the reasons for this free stress is that English has freely borrowed words from many languages and has retained the stress pattern of the source language.

Stress is responsible for rhythm in language. Rhythm is based on difference in energy which foregrounds some syllables. In English rhythm depends on the occurrence of stressed and unstressed syllables. English is a stress-timed language while some other languages are syllable-timed. This means that in English all the syllables in an utterance are not stressed and therefore the time taken in completing an utterance will depend on the number of stressed syllables since, we know, a stressed syllable takes more time than an unstressed one to utter. In some other languages, French, for example, all the syllables in an utterance are stressed. So the time taken in completing an utterance will depend on the number of syllables in it. These languages are known as syllable-timed. In English stressed and unstressed syllables in an utterance occur at equal intervals of time. In order to achieve this, unstressed syllables are compressed or reduced in some way, some consonants are deleted and vowels are pronounced as either /ɪ/ or /ə/. For example, 'fun and food' becomes 'fun n food', 'bread and butter' is spoken as 'bread n butter', in 'absent' (noun) the vowel in the second syllable becomes a neutral vowel or schwa. This is also achieved by using the weakened and contracted forms of certain classes of words like determiners, prepositions, auxiliary verbs or the negative marker 'not'. If there is a sequence of unstressed syllables one of the weak syllables is deleted, for example, 'comparable' is pronounced as /kɒmprəbl/ or 'national' is pronounced as /næʃnəl/ deleting the second syllable in both words.

7.5 Some Rules for Locating the Stressed Syllable in English

The speakers of English have a tendency to avoid having stresses too close to each other. This may cause the stress on a polysyllabic word to be on one syllable in one sentence and on another in another sentence. Ladefoged gives the following examples: 'He had a clarinet' with stress on the first syllable of 'clarinet' and 'He plays the clarinet' with stress on the second syllable of 'clarinet', 'Vice-president Jones' with stress on Vice and Jones and 'Jones, the Vice-president' with stress on Jones and president. Numerals like 15, 16, 17, etc. are stressed on the first syllable but in a sentence like He is only 'sixteen' it is the second syllable of 'sixteen' which is stressed. The interval between stresses is affected by the number of syllables within the stress group and by the number and type of vowels and consonants within each syllable.

We have seen that stress in English is free as well as fixed. This can cause some problem in locating the stressed syllable in a word which may sometimes lead to loss or confusion of meaning. We have also seen that a learner of the language has to learn the stress pattern in individual words separately. However, there are some easy rules which can help the learner locate the stressed syllable in disyllabic or polysyllabic words.

(a) Words formed by adding to a word of common use a prefix having a distinct meaning of its own have usually two strong stresses, a stress on the prefix and a stress on the stem or the root. Some examples are: anti-, arch-, dis- (meaning separate), ex- (meaning former), half-, joint-, in- (il-, im-, ir-), inter- (meaning reciprocal), mal-, mis- (meaning error), non-, out-, over- (meaning too much), pre- (meaning before), re- (meaning again, repetition), sub- (meaning subordinate), ultra-, un-, under- and vice-.

(b) Words formed by adding the suffixes -ing, -ious, -ous, -er, etc. do not change the stress pattern of the root or the stem. Example: 'beˈgin-beginning-beˈginner', 'grace-ˈgracious'.

(c) Words ending in -ical, -ically have the stress on the preceding syllable. Example: 'poˈlitical', 'poˈlitically'.

(d) Words ending in -ic, -ics have stress on the syllable preceding these endings. Examples: 'acaˈdemic', 'ecoˈnomics'.

(e) Words ending in -ity have stress on the syllable preceding the ending. Example: 'pubˈlicity'.

(f) Words ending in -ique, -ee, -eer, -ese and -ette have stress on the syllable containing these endings. Example: uˈnique, emploˈyee, engiˈneer, oˈbese, cigarˈette, etc.

(g) Words ending in -ate are stressed on the third syllable from the end. Example: ˈeducate, ˈinculcate, etc.

(h) Words ending in -ion have stress on the syllable preceding this ending. Example: exami'nation, 'friction, etc.

(i) Double stress is used in compound adjectives of which the first element is also an adjective. Example: 'red 'hot.

(j) Reflexive pronouns, that is pronouns with 'self' or 'selves', are stressed on the syllables containing these endings. Example: my'self, our'selves, etc.

(k) Stress is also marked on the basis of grammatical category and function of words, nouns and adjectives generally have stress on the first syllable while verbs have stress on the second syllable. Example: insult (n) has stress on the first syllable but insult (v) has stress on the second syllable. This may result in change/weakening of the vowel which loses the stress.

Example:	Noun/Adjective	Verb
	'Absent	Ab'sent
	'Transfer	Trans'fer

(l) In connected speech structure words are not stressed. Usually the vowel is weakened or the word is shortened. Example: I have read this book – I've read this book. It is the content words which receive stress unless special emphasis is required to be given to the structure word to convey the intended meaning.

7.6 Stress in the Speech of Indian Speakers

Indian speakers usually put stress on the last syllable of the word. Sometimes the stressed syllable is altogether missed out as in the word 'develop' which is usually pronounced by many people as 'devlop' leaving out '-ve' the stressed syllable and stressing '-de' which is unstressed in the speech of native speakers. R.K. Bansal in Spoken English For India cites many interesting examples of misplaced stress and the effect they have on communication of meaning. Readers may refer to the book.

Exercise

1. What do you understand by the term stress?
2. Discuss the functions of stress and give examples.
3. Stress in English is free as well as fixed. Elaborate and exemplify.
4. Fill in the blank spaces with appropriate words.
   (a) There are ...... degrees of stress.
   (b) Voiced sounds have .... vibration in stressed syllables.
   (c) The length of the vowel in the stressed syllable ....
   (d) Vowels in stressed syllables are ....
   (e) The syllable which receives greater degree of force is the .... syllable.
   (f) Words ending in -ate are stressed on the ...... syllable from the end.
   (g) Nouns and adjectives generally have stress on the .... syllable.

8

Intonation

In the previous chapter, we saw how words are spoken in isolation. For the correct or the intended meaning of the word to be expressed it must be stressed on the right syllable. There is another supra-segmental feature which contributes to meaning. This is an essential feature of connected speech. This feature is known as intonation.

8.1 Introduction

In connected speech all the words do not receive equal importance. One word stands out from the rest and the stressed syllable in this word receives greater prominence because of more rapid pitch change. This is known as intonation. Stress and intonation are, therefore, inter-linked and work together to give the effect of prominence. According to Ladefoged, the intonation of a sentence is the pattern of pitch changes that occurs. Let us now look at the sentence 'We are ˈdoing PhoˈnetIcs'. In this sentence spoken in the normal way we have two stressed syllables, 'ˈdo' and 'ˈne'. Since Phonetics is the most important word here, so the stressed syllable in this word receives the effect of pitch change. However, it is possible to change the pitch on 'we', 'are' and 'do' depending on what we want to emphasize. But-ing of 'doing' can never be given prominence because it can never be a stressed syllable. Intonation is affected by the speaker's emotion and degree of intensity. Greater change and range of pitch is observed if there is greater intensity. The syllable which receives the effect of pitch change is called the nucleus or the nuclear syllable. It is also known as the tonic syllable. So in the above example 'ne' is the nucleus or the tonic syllable.

8.2 Types of Intonation

The tone used by a speaker can either be level or static or moving or kinetic.

(a) Level tone is used in prayers, counting, etc. It is known as monotone. It can either be high or low. High tone is indicated by placing a vertical bar above and before the stressed syllables and low tone is indicated by placing the bar below and before the stressed syllables.

(b) Kinetic or moving tone is that which uses greater pitch change and highlights some fact in the utterance. It can be falling, rising, falling-rising and rising-falling. Falling tone is indicated by placing a slanting bar above and before the nuclear syllable, rising tone by placing this bar in a reverse manner, that is, below and before the nuclear syllable, falling-rising by joining the two bars and placing it before and above the nuclear syllable and the rising-falling by reversing it and placing it above and before the nuclear syllable. The following diagram will make it clear.

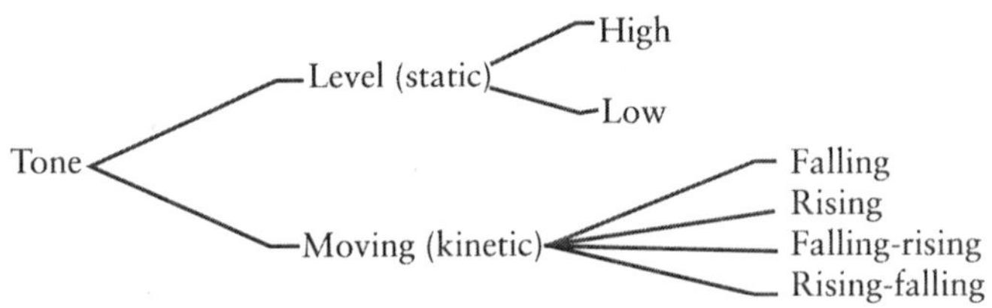

8.3 Group

Let us look at the utterance 'When the teacher arrived, we all stood up'. We cannot utter the sentence together. So it is broken into two parts—'when the teacher arrived' and 'we all stood up'. These parts are known as groups. These are also known as tone groups, breath groups or sense groups.

There are various other names also by which it is known. Some of these names are tone-units, phonemic clause and intonation phrase. The groups are determined on the basis of physiological, syntactic and semantic factors. According to Ladefoged, the way in which a speaker breaks up a sentence depends largely on what that person considers to be important information points in the sentence. A tone group is a unit of information rather than a syntactically defined unit. M.A.K. Halliday also thinks that 'a tone unit is one unit of information'. Each group has a nuclear or tonic syllable and, as we have seen, pitch change takes place here. The above utterance has been divided into two groups and the most important syllables in the groups have been marked by putting an appropriate mark. These are the syllables which receive the effect of pitch change. Group division is shown by placing a slanting line between the groups. A semicolon, a colon and a full stop always mark the end of a group and a comma usually marks it. Distribution of meaning or grammatical structure also determines a tone group.

8.4 Functions of Intonation

Intonation can have either accentual or non-accentual function. It is used for accentual function in order to highlight prominent parts of an utterance. The non-accentual function of intonation is to indicate the mood or the attitude of the speaker to the listener or topic or to show the speaker's personality. It is also used for the purpose of distinguishing types of sentences, that is, for grammatical purpose. In its grammatical function it also indicates the exact kind of subordination of a relative clause to its main clause. The relative clause can either be defining or non-defining. It functions as a defining clause if it forms a part of the same tone group as its antecedent. But if it forms a separate tone group, it functions as a non-defining relative clause. The following example will make it clear.

(i) My friend who lives in Mysore is arriving tomorrow.

(ii) My friend, who lives in Mysore, is arriving tomorrow.

The first sentence has a defining relative clause 'who lives in Mysore' and so it will be a part of the tone group of its antecedent 'My friend' and will be marked thus 'My friend who lives in Mysore/is arriving tomorrow.' The second has a non-defining relative clause 'who lives in Mysore' and so it will form a separate group. It will be marked as 'My friend/ who lives in Mysore/is coming tomorrow.' (A defining relative clause restricts the meaning of the noun it qualifies while a non-defining relative clause merely gives some additional information about the noun it qualifies.)

In its non-accentual function it can be objective or syntactic or grammatical and subjective and indicate mood, attitude, etc. The different intonation patterns described above perform the above functions.

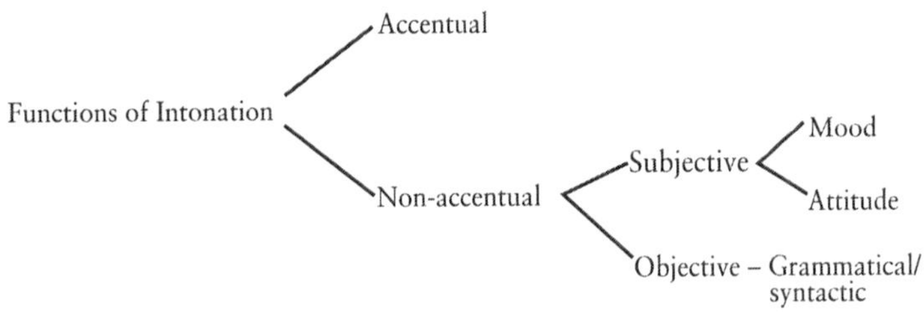

Let us now look at the different accentual and non-accentual functions of the kinetic tones.

8.4.1 Falling Tone

The falling tone is used for the following purposes.

(a) The falling tone is used in utterances which are statements made in an uncoloured manner, that is, without any implied meaning. It is used for the sheer purpose of passing on some information to the listener. The statement 'My friend left for home yesterday' spoken with a falling intonation simply passes on some information about the speaker's friend to the listener.

(b) The falling tone is also used for utterances that are commands. For example, when the master says 'Finish the work by noon', he is issuing a command and therefore using the falling tone.

(c) Wh-questions asked in a neutral, matter-of-fact way are spoken with falling intonation. For example, when someone asks 'Where do you live?' only in order to know the place of residence of the listener and for no other reasons the tone has to be the falling tone.

(d) Tag questions, that is, questions which follow a statement and form part of the same sentence, can be asked either for confirmation of the statement or for seeking opinion. If they are asked for the former purpose the speaker uses the falling intonation. For example, if someone says 'The boy is very intelligent, isn't he?' with falling intonation, he is merely trying to get an affirmation of the statement he has made about the boy.

(e) Exclamations are yet another type of sentences for which falling intonation is used. For example, 'What a wonderful day!' or 'How nice of you!' are exclamations and spoken with the falling tone.

(f) When the speaker comes to the end of an utterance which has two or more tone groups, that is when the utterance is completed, the falling tone is used. For example, in 'When I reached his home, he was sleeping' 'sleeping' marks the end of the utterance and so the falling tone is used marking finality or completion.

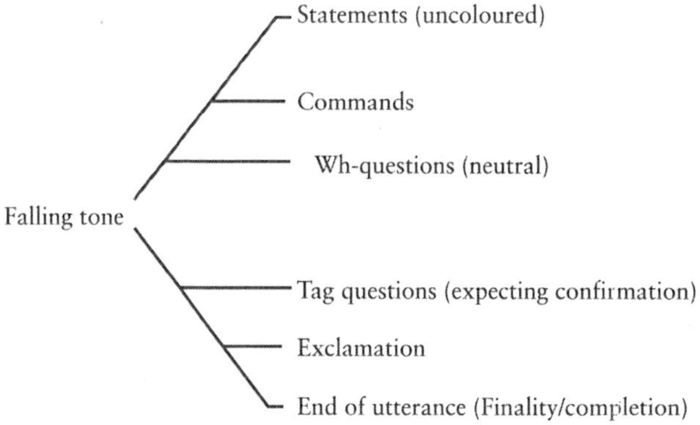

8.4.2 Rising Tone

Rising tone has the following functions.

(a) It is used in a tone group which does not complete an utterance. In the example in 8.4.1.6 'When I reached his home, he was sleeping.' There are two tone groups. The first ends at 'home' but it does not complete the utterance. Therefore rising tone will be used to indicate that the utterance is not complete and there is something more that follows.

(b) Yes/no type of direct questions, that is questions eliciting either yes or no as reply, are spoken with a rising tone. Such questions begin with an auxiliary verb. So questions like 'Are you coming this evening?' will be spoken with a rising tone.

(c) Wh-type of questions spoken in a polite and friendly manner warrant the use of rising tone as opposed to the wh-questions asked merely to elicit some information. For example, when we ask a child 'What is your name?' we use the rising tone in order to sound friendly and familiar.

(d) Polite requests, apology, expression of sorrow or sympathy also require the use of rising tone.

(e) Rising tone is also used in tag questions when the speaker is not sure of the answer as opposed to the tag questions which expect confirmation of the statement. So a tag question like 'He's coming tomorrow, isn't he?' spoken with the rising tone indicates that the speaker is not sure of the fact.

(f) Complaints are expressed by using the rising tone. For example, a sentence like 'You didn't tell me' spoken with the rising tone conveys the speaker's annoyance at the fact that he was not informed about certain thing though he expected to be informed.

(g) Expressions like 'good night' or 'bye' etc. are spoken with the rising tone.

(h) An utterance which is syntactically a statement can be used to ask a question if instead of using the falling tone rising tone is used. Thus, the sentence 'You are going home' which is syntactically a statement will become a question if instead of the falling tone rising tone is used.

Rising tone
- Incomplete utterance
- Yes/No question
- Wh-questions (polite and friendly)
- Polite requests
- Tag question (when the answer is not certain)
- Complaint
- Greetings at parting
- Statements (meant to be yes/no type of question)

8.4.3 Falling-rising Tone

The falling-rising pattern of intonation is used for the following purposes.

(a) The falling-rising tone is used when the utterance has some implication. This means that there is more to it than meets the eye or rather the ear. Insinuations, veiled threats, apology, unpleasant news, happiness, doubt, reassurance, etc. are some of the meanings which are expressed by the use of this tone. A sentence like 'I didn't mean this.' will be a statement if spoken with the falling tone but will express apology if the falling-rising tone is used. Similarly 'He's coming tomorrow.' spoken with the falling tone will be a matter-of-fact statement but when spoken with the falling-rising tone express happiness and pleasant surprise.

(b) This intonation pattern is also used to indicate contrast. 'He's intelligent but lazy.' spoken with this tone at the end of the second tone group will imply contrast.

(c) Another function of this tone is to express encouragement. For example, the sentence 'It's all right.' spoken with this tone tries to encourage the listener.

(d) Expression of hope is yet another function of this tone. For example, 'I hope it doesn't rain' spoken with this tone will express hope on the part of the speaker.

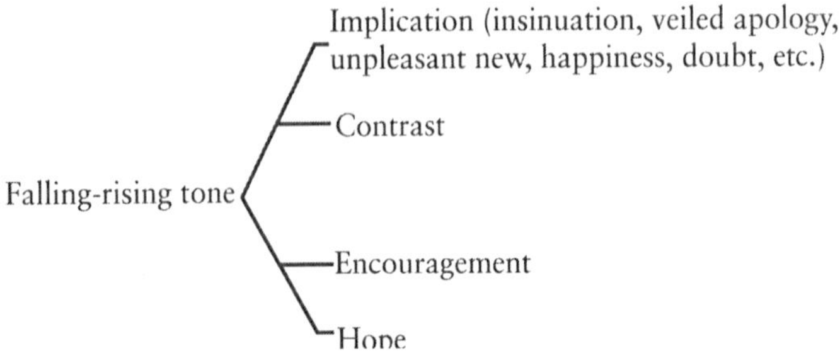

8.4.4 The Rising-falling Tone

This intonation pattern is not very common and is not used in English. However, it can perform the following functions.

(a) It is used to indicate enthusiastic agreement.

(b) Another function of this tone is to indicate certainty as opposed to doubt.

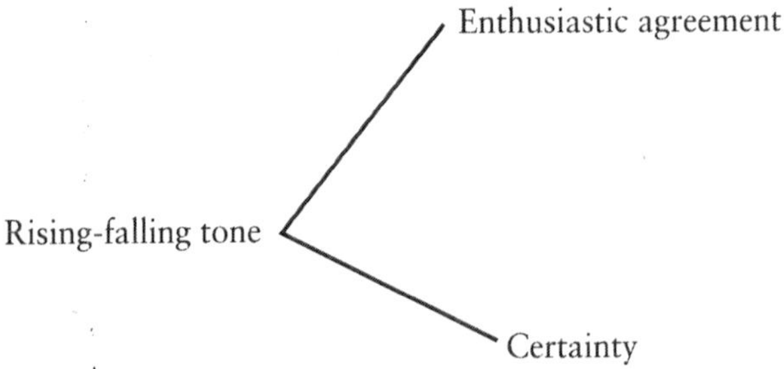

8.5 Divided Nucleus

In the case of the last two intonation patterns the pitch change can take place either on one syllable or on two different syllables. In the latter case the nucleus is called divided nucleus as in 'The weather is good' where the falling tone is on 'weather' and the rising on 'good'.

8.6 Placing the Nucleus and Marking the other Stressed Syllables

It is usually the last most important syllable in a group that receives the effect of pitch change and so it is the nucleus. However, for reasons of emphasis (accentual function) some other syllable may be given prominence. When spoken in the normal way the pitch change in the sentence 'I asked him to come tomorrow' will take place on the second syllable of 'tomorrow' because this is the last most important syllable in the sentence. In this case the other stressed syllables before the syllable receiving the effect of pitch change will be marked by placing a vertical bar above and before these stressed syllables as is normally done to indicate primary stress. But if prominence is to be given to 'I' then pitch change will take place here and the stressed syllables after this will be marked by placing the vertical bar below and before these stressed syllables as is done to indicate secondary stress. The sentence will now be spoken as 'I asked him to come tomorrow.' We must also notice that 'I' was unstressed in the former case. There are three parts of a tone group, namely, head, pre-head and tail. Head is the stretch beginning with the first stressed syllable known as head onset and extending up to the nucleus, pre-head is constituted of unstressed syllable preceding the head and tail comprises the unstressed syllable or syllables after the nucleus and before the next tone group boundary.

The intonation patterns discussed above are not the same for R.P. and non-R.P. speakers. R.P. model may not be useful in analyzing the intonation of non-R.P. regional varieties of English.

8.7 Intonation in the Speech of Indian Speakers

Indian speakers by and large follow these intonation patterns because they are universal in nature.

Exercise

1. What is intonation? What are the different intonation patterns? Answer with examples.

2. What do you understand by the term group? How is an utterance divided into groups?
3. What are the different types of function of intonation?
4. Discuss the functions of the falling tone and give examples.
5. Discuss the functions of the rising tone and give examples.
6. Discuss the functions of the falling-rising tone and give examples.
7. Discuss the functions of the rising-falling tone and give examples.
8. How is the nucleus placed in a tone group and how are the other stressed syllables marked in the group? Answer with examples.
9. Fill in the blanks with the correct word.
   (a) There are ...... distinct intonation patterns.
   (b) Uncoloured statements are spoken with the .... intonation.
   (c) The falling tone marks the .... of an utterance.
   (d) Polite and friendly Wh-type of questions are spoken with the .... tone.
   (e) Complaints are expressed by using the .... tone.
   (f) The falling-rising tone expresses ....
   (g) In its subjective function intonation identifies the .... and ...... attitude of the speaker.
   (h) Intonation is affected by the speaker's .... and degree of ....

9

Features of Connected Speech

The speech act is a continuum and not just stringing together discrete linguistic units like phonemes, syllables, words and phrases. In the process of the act some sounds undergo a change and sometimes they get deleted or are connected to a sound in the neighbouring word. These are features of connected speech which, instead of affecting intelligibility, help it. We shall now look at these features and their role in connected speech.

9.1 Assimilation

In connected speech all the syllables and words are not always spoken in the same way as they are spoken in isolation. Sometimes a sound in a syllable, a morpheme or a word is influenced by the sound of a syllable, morpheme or word preceding or following it. The way in which sounds are influenced by each other is called assimilation. For example, when 'one' and 'pound' are spoken together, the dental /n/ changes into bilabial /m/ under the influence of the following bilabial sound /p/ in 'pound'. In the word 'newspaper' the voiced /z/ of 'news' changes into voiceless /s/ because the following sound /p/ is a voiceless sound. It is clear from the above examples that it is the consonants which are affected by the process of assimilation. Vowels also undergo change. Some vowels are weakened, but this happens when the syllable in which they occur lose stress. Sometimes vowel change also takes place when new words are formed from existing words, for example, 'nation-national'. These cases are not examples of assimilation because the change does not take place under the influence of the neighbouring sound.

The assimilatory changes taking place can either be phonemic or allophonic. When we speak 'his son' /hiz sʌ n/ as /his sʌ n/ the assimilatory change is allophonic because voiced /z/ changes into devoiced /z/ under the influence of the following voiceless sound in 'son'. But when in 'one pound' /n/ of 'one' is changed into /m/ under the influence of bilabial /p/ the change is phonemic because /n/ and /m/ are two different phonemes in English. Since every language has its own stock of phonemes and their allophones, what is phonemic in one language may be allophonic in another language and what is allophonic in one language may be phonemic in another.

9.1.1 Types of Assimilation

The assimilatory change takes place either inside a word or at word boundary. If it occurs at word boundary it is known as juxtapositional assimilation as in our example 'one pound'. As we have seen the process of assimilation affects both the preceding and following sounds in different situations. In our example of 'newspaper' the preceding sound is influenced by the following sound. But when we pronounce /l/ a voiced sound as devoiced as in the words 'play', 'clay', etc., the devoicing is the result of the influence of the preceding sound which is voiceless. The type of assimilation where the preceding sound is affected by the following sound is called anticipatory or regressive assimilation and when the following sound is affected it is called progressive or preservative assimilation.

In some cases we find a different kind of assimilation. The word 'attract' is pronounced as /at^{h}rækt/. Here the alveolar /t/ becomes post-alveolar because the following /r/ is post-alveolar and at the same time /r/ which is voiced becomes voiceless under the influence of the voiceless /t/.

Types of assimilation

- Anticipatory/Regressive: Preceding sound affected by the following one
- Progressive: Following sound affected by the preceding one
- Two way assimilation: Both preceding and following sounds affected

Thus both the preceding and the following sounds are affected in this example. This is called two way assimilation.

If we look at the above account of assimilation we shall find that the process of assimilation can affect the place of articulation as in the case of /n/ changing into /m/ in 'one pound', manner of articulation as in /d/ becoming /n/ in 'good night' which many people speak as /gunnight/ where a plosive becomes a nasal, or voicing as the voiced /l/ becoming voiceless/ devoiced as in 'play'. The second case is found mainly in the most rapid casual speech.

Assimilation, it may be noted, is not a compulsory feature in a number of languages. English does not also observe it in an obligatory manner. This means that it depends on the speaker whether he chooses to observe it or not in his speech. However, the process of assimilation enables the speaker to achieve economy of effort in the sequence of words. It results in reducing the number or extent of the adjustments which the speech organs have to perform while moving from one word or one sound to the next. This effort-saving process depends on three types of changes in the sequence of movements which produce speech. They are (1) changes involving the state of the glottis, (2) changes involving action of the velum and (3) changes involving movement of the articulators. In the first type of change a voiceless sound becomes voiced under the influence of the neighbouring voiced sound and a voiceless sound becomes voiced because the neighbouring sound is voiced. Thus 'birthday' may be spoken as 'bird day', 'blackboard' as 'blagboard'. It is generally regressive. Similarly, one may speak 'of course' as 'ov course' and 'what's' as 'what is'. In the first example a voiced sound /v/ changes into a voiceless sound /f/ because the neighbouring sound /k/ is voiceless and /z/, a voiced sound changes into /s/ which is voiceless. Changes resulting in this kind of assimilation can be both progressive and regressive as we have seen in the examples above. The most frequent type of assimilation in English is that in which articulators are involved. The frequency of this type of assimilation increases as the speech becomes more rapid and familiar. These assimilations are generally regressive: 'one pound' becomes 'ome pound'.

Assimilation can also be either complete or partial. When assimilation is complete one sound completely changes into another as in the example in the previous sentence. In partial assimilation we get two states of the glottis working together and the voiced sound becomes whispered. This type of assimilation is found commonly in English and can be both regressive and progressive. One other feature of this type of assimilation is that it almost always involves either plosives or fricatives.

There is yet another kind of assimilation which is found in languages. Over a period of time a sound may change its features and acquire the features of the neighbouring sound. This can be both regressive and progressive. As an example of this kind of assimilation we can cite the change that gives us the present pronunciation of 'orchard' which was originally 'ort+yard'. Strictly speaking, the study of this kind of assimilation is the concern of historical linguistics.

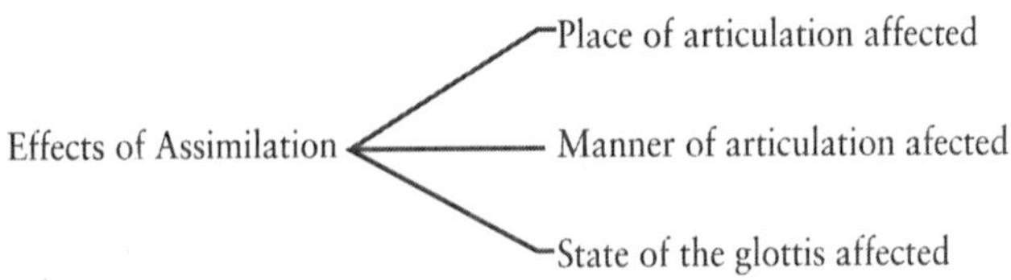

9.2 Elision

We saw in 7.3 that sometimes in rapid speech some sounds are dropped without affecting the meaning of the utterance.

For example, instead of saying 'How kind of you!' we say /haUkaɪ ndəjU/ dropping the final /v/ sound of 'of'. This is known as elision. However, this is found in the most casual speech. In formal speech speakers are required to produce all the sounds.

9.2.1 Types of Elision

Elision can be of the following types.

(a) Weak vowels are lost after /p/, /t/ /k/ as in 'tomato', pronounced as /ʰtəmɑ:təU/, 'canary' pronounced as /ʰkneərɪ/, etc.

(b) /n/, /t/ and /r/ become syllabic when preceded by a weak vowel which is dropped as in 'tonight' becoming /tnaɪt/, 'police' becoming /pli:s/ or 'correct' becoming /krekt/.

(c) In some other case the last sound of a word or syllable gets dropped as in 'fast track' becoming /fa:stræk/, 'good bye' becoming /gUbaɪ/, 'recognize' becoming /rekʌnaɪz/.

(d) In casual rapid speech /v/ of 'of' is usually dropped and so we speak 'waste of time' as /weɪstətaɪm/.

(e) Contraction constitutes a very common feature of connected speech. In informal connected speech we say 'I can't do' instead of 'I cannot do' or 'I've read it' instead of 'I have read it.' This is yet another example of elision. Usually it is the auxiliary verbs and the negative marker 'not' which get contracted.

9.3 Liaison

Another feature of connected speech is liaison. In connected speech, we have seen, we do not produce the sounds as discrete units; they are produced in a continuum. Thus the utterance 'at all' is pronounced in such a way that /t/ of 'at' and /ɔ:/ of 'all' get juxtaposed or liaised and we pronounce it as /ətʰɔ: l/ and not as /æt ɔ: l/. We have seen how the letter 'r' is pronounced when it occurs at the end of a word and the next word begins with a vowel, or how we pronounce 'r' sound when a word ends in a vowel and the following word also begins with a vowel. These are all examples of liaison.

9.4 Juncture

Two words with identical sounds can be spoken in two different ways to signal two different meanings. We may pause briefly either at one sound or the other. If the two sounds come in succession and the pause is not at the right sound, communication can suffer. Let us look at the following: 'ice cream-I scream'. In the first word we cannot pause after /aɪ/ and before 's' but can do so after 's' of 'ice' and before 'k' of cream. If this is not done meaning is affected. In 'I scream' we cannot pause between the sounds /s/ and /k/ but we have to pause between /aɪ/ and /s/ of 'scream' for correct communication. This is known as juncture. If the location of syllable juncture is changed from one point to another, the meaning will completely change. Some examples given by Gimson are as follows: 'pea stalks – peace talks', 'a name – an aim', 'that stuff – that's tough', 'the way to cut it – the waiter cut it' and 'how strained – house trained', 'why choose – white shoes'.

In phonetic transcription correct syllable juncture can be indicated by putting a dot (.) between the syllables where juncture is required.

9.4.1 Types of Juncture

Juncture is of two types: (i) open juncture and (ii) close juncture.

(a) *Open Juncture*: When there is a slight pause between two sounds it is called open juncture. In the example in 9.4, there is open juncture between /aɪ/ and 's' of 'scream'.

(b) In the other example 'Ice cream' there is no pause between /aɪ/ and 'c' of 'ice'. This is known as close juncture.

Juncture
- Open: some pause between two sounds
- Close: no pause between two sounds

9.5 Features of Connected Speech in Indian English

The features discussed above are generally not found in the speech of Indian speakers of English and it does not also cause any problem in communication. However, for more effective and better communication with native speakers it may help if these features are acquired.

Exercise

1. What is assimilation? Give examples.
2. Write notes on (i) anticipatory assimilation, (ii) progressive assimilation and (iii) two way assimilation.
3. How does assimilation affect the assimilated sounds? Discuss with examples.
4. Discuss the uses and types of elision with examples.
5. Why are assimilation, elision and liaison used by speakers?
6. In what way does juncture help in the communication of meaning? Answer with examples.
7. Say whether the following statements are true or false.
   (a) Assimilation helps economy of effort.

   True False

   (b) Juxtapositional assimilation occurs at syllable boundary.

   True False

   (c) Anticipatory assimilation affects the preceding sound.

   True False

(d) There are no examples of two way assimilation in English.

True False

(e) Assimilation is not compulsory in many languages including English.

True False

(f) In connected speech shifting of syllable juncture does not alter the meaning.

True False

(g) Assimilation can affect the place of articulation, the manner of articulation and also the state of the glottis.

True False

10

Varieties of English Pronunciation and the Need for a Model

Plurality, heterogeneity and diversity are frequently used terms that largely define the enormity of current global trends. The domain of life has expanded unimaginably as ultramodern gadgets have substantially minimized the range of time and space. To exemplify it, a smart mobile removes the barrier of distance between two people sitting in two different continents who may conveniently exchange a variety of experiences through audio-visual signals within no time. The concept of whole world as a global village is a reality now and it has immensely enhanced the aspirations and dreams of mankind. An individual wishes to explore all sorts of possibilities cutting across the geographical boundary that may ensure the quality of life. With the help of modern appliances, mankind has adequately succeeded in making different components of the universe accessible. This overwhelming accessibility of mankind to the diversity of nature has necessitated the emergence of a global language. Under these unprecedented circumstances, the expansion of English language is also taking place contributing to its diversified usage.

10.1 Emergence of Varieties and Globalization

The degree of expansion of English at global level has resulted into outnumbering of its native speakers by non-native speakers (Crystal, 2003). The situation is that out of every four speaker of English, only one is a native speaker. Almost 80 per cent of the communication in English as a foreign or second language does not involve the role of a native speaker (Beneke, 1991). It is an undeniable fact that no other language has ever shown such a high degree of social penetration and acceptance as English during the last three to four decades. In such a situation it would not be out of context to establish that the real ownership of English appears to be slipping from the clutches of its native speakers. The writers of English coming from non-native background are getting recognition as they are frequently walking away with prestigious literary awards leaving behind the native writers in competition. It indicates that there has been qualitative expansion of English across the globe. It is this phenomenon that has led to emergence of Commonwealth, Subaltern and Black literature, etc. with predominant use of the English language. England freed its colonies but left English as one of the influencial languages of these colonies with a high degree of penetration into their socio-cultural domain. The people of these newly emerging nations had new hopes, aspirations and euphoria to come up in life. At the same time, the wounds of exploitation, oppression and discrimination needed nursing through their recounting in the form of native literature. Though English carried the stigmatic imprint of colonizers, its deep assimilation and adaptation in the social fabric resisted the sense of aversion towards it among people in general. Their hatred towards this language partly subsided due to its strong support of contemporary intelligentsia and elite section as these people viewed English as the language of technological advancement and upward social mobility. These factors did not stop people from using English but promoted them to use it in a form that strongly accommodated the native elements of these countries, such as, vocabulary, idioms and structures that suited their sensibility. Consequently, this phenomenon led to the emergence of new varieties of English. A glance at Indo-Anglian writings can stand witness to these claims where we find copious use of native elements. The poems of Toru Datta, Sri Aurobindo, Sarojini Naidu, etc. seem to be filtered through Indianness in many respects. It is not only overwhelming contents that constitute the thematic aspects wrapped in nativity, even nomenclature and melody remain rooted in Indian ethos. The titles like 'Savitri', 'Songs of Radha', 'The Milkmaid', 'Vrindavan', etc. by Indian poets are evident of such attempts of nativization. It would not be an overemphasis to state that this drive of nativization has infused fresh interest among readers that has, in turn, contributed to the strengthening of roots of English in Indian soil. At phonological level, this phenomenon necessitated interaction between English and Hindi sounds, the effect of which has been adequately discussed in Chapter 5 under the heading "Salient Features of Indian English".

Today, English is overwhelmingly used in developing and underdeveloped third world countries for different purposes in areas like tourism, economy, technology, academics and what not. Native English speaking countries are warmly receiving different varieties of English coming up in other countries by accommodating words taken from these varieties in the standard dictionaries published by Oxford and Cambridge Universities in the upgraded editions. Here, it is relevant to mention that the impulse of globalization is largely shaped by consumerist attitude where all affairs are settled among different nations in terms of mechanics of gain and loss. The sphere of knowledge has also not remained untouched by it as all publishing houses vie with each other for promoting their sale even at the expense of quality. The concept of standard has altogether become highly subjective and quality is evaluated in terms of profitability of the firms that depend on innumerable variables like advertisement, consumer's mental ability and affordability, socio-cultural scenario where the product is to be marketed, etc. The situation has changed so much so that the standard of a product is largely determined by market forces rather than the exquisite intrinsic quality of the product. This ultra-modern, technology-driven global society is virtually redefining the traditional concept of standard by incorporating in it the elements of instant gratification and excess of utilitarian concerns. It is a stark reality that the change in concepts of time and space has left its imprint on our verbal behaviour too, that is to be displayed at global platform. The concept of Standard English, from this perspective, has undergone substantial modification as the consumerist attitude has gobbled up the nuances of subtle communication skills. The adherence to such nuances of the Standard English has been replaced by utterly utilitarian motives of communicators where premium is laid only on successful exchange of ideas, i.e., intelligibility that turns out to be the source of instant gratification. The young generation of our society that is the real engine and architect of modern global design nourishes this attitude that has forced the idea of conforming to the standard of English to the back seat. This trend of global communication has provided ample space to a large number of varieties of English to flourish which are popularly called global Englishes.

Conventionally, non-native English speaking countries have a variety of English that bears the influence of their mother tongues. In all such countries, communicative needs in English inside a geographical boundary are fulfilled without conforming to any well-established and globally recognized standard pronunciation. In a highly industrialized and mechanical world dominated by consumerism, people rarely look for sophistication and elegance in pronunciation. This mechanical approach to communication has resulted into the dilution of effort required to conform to standard pronunciation on one hand and the emergence of a number of varieties in due course on the other hand. The situation is that in each non-native country where English is used for a reasonably good number of purposes, a particular variety has originated depending on the mother tongue influence. For instance, in India we have Indian English with distinct phonological features caused by the pull of mother tongue, that is Hindi, for a large majority of Indians. Likewise we have Nigerian English, Indonesian English, Malaysian English, Sudanese English, Singhalese English, where each of these varieties has developed under the effect of mother tongue of the speakers. All of these varieties show their distinctive phonological features when compared to the Standard English pronunciation. Here, it is important to clarify that all the phonological features (segmental and supra-segmental) of English language dealt with in this book have been described, analyzed and explained keeping in view the parameters of standard English pronunciation, i.e. BBC English/Received Pronunciation (R.P.). The deviations from these parameters determine the identity of different varieties. In order to have a systematic study of these varieties, we may divide these varieties into two broad headings: Native-English variety and Non-native English variety. Native English variety includes those varieties of English which are used as mother tongue, that is to say, in English speaking countries like Canada, Australia, America, etc. Non-native English variety consists of those varieties of English which developed as second language in countries like India, South Africa, Nigeria, etc.

All these countries were at certain points of time the colonies of England. Therefore, the British colonialism has been the most important factor behind the expansion of English that eventually paved the way for emergence of its varieties. Native-English variety evolved in those countries where there was absence of a predominant form of native language. It gave the colonizers an adequate opportunity to introduce English that finally established itself as the national language with passage of time. In a country like India or South Africa, it could not be possible because these countries had their own well-developed forms of languages with which their natives were emotionally attached. Hence, English could not replace these native languages but succeeded in creating viable space for itself. Later on, people of these colonies realized the inevitability of English in a rapidly growing world and accepted it as a resource for progress. After decolonization of these countries, a wave of protest against imperial English started as many nationalists took it as an imprint of their slavery. But this protest could not catch considerable momentum in native-English speaking countries as it turned out to be a very daunting task for people to find out a viable alternative of English language all on a sudden and throwing away of English also meant distancing from the mainstream of advancement. These challenges forced the protesters to go ahead with colonial English that occupied the place of native language. In non-native English speaking countries, the protesters' voice was stifled taking into account the utilitarian concerns of imperial English where it occupied the status of a second language as is the case of English in India.

10.2 Features of American English

It would not be out of context to mention here that America got freedom from British rule in 1776 and emerged as a major global force by the late 19th century. American people were highly charged with nationalistic spirit and fervour. Some of them looked at English as the symbol of colonial rule and so wanted to get rid of it. A group of intellectuals led by Webster stood in support of this view. They advocated for a separate variety of English that may have American imprint. Consequently, American academicians and linguists adopted several modifications in the existing imperial English at different linguistic levels such as morphological (word level), phonological (sound level), syntactic (sentence level) and semantic (meaning level), etc. These linguistic innovations under the growing influence of America as the global leader firmly established a new variety of English that is popularly known as American English. Let us see how distinct these modifications are compared to the Standard British English (R.P.).

(a) In American English, /r/ sound is pronounced when it occurs at the end as in /car/, /scare/, /major/, etc., or after a vowel and before a consonant sound as in /market/, /first/, /smart/, etc. This sound is not pronounced in the Standard British English in the positions given above. Technically, this phenomenon is called rhoticism and thus, American English is marked by rhotic accent.

(b) In American English, /æ/ sound is pronounced in the place of /a:/ of the Standard British English. For example, the words 'pass' /pa:s/, 'ask' /a:sk/, 'staff' /sta:f/, etc. of the Standard British English are pronounced as /pæs/, /æsk/ and /stæf/ respectively in American English.

(c) Many disyllabic words, especially loan words from French, get stress on the second syllable in American English whereas it is laid on the first syllable in British English. For instance, in the words like 'brochure', 'adult', 'chauffeur', etc. first syllable is stressed in British English but in American English the second syllable is stressed. Further, in the case of disyllabic verbs like 'dictate', 'migrate', 'locate' that end in '-ate', stress is laid on the first syllable in American English while the second syllable is stressed in these words in British English.

(d) Diphthongs used in British English are usually realized as monophthongs in American English as seen in the words like 'take', 'coat', 'note', etc.

(e) The vowel /ɒ/ pronounced in the British English is transformed into /a:/ in American English in the words like 'college', 'commerce', 'not', etc. In British English, lip rounding is required during articulation of such words, whereas this lip rounding is missing in American English during the pronunciation of such words.

(f) In American English, vowels in certain phonetic environment are shortened to a very large extent unlike the case in British English. For example, the last syllable in words like 'crocodile', 'fertile', etc. are pronounced as /daIl/ in British English but these are pronounced as /dl/ in American English as the vowels in them are shortened extremely.

(g) /j/ sound that occurs before /u:/ sound in some words like 'tune' /tju:n/, 'new' /nju:/, 'student' /stju:dənt/, etc. in British English is dropped in American English where these words are pronounced as /tu:n/, /nu:/ and /stu:dənt/ respectively.

All of these features show the degree of distinction of American English from the Standard British English at the level of phonology that is the central concern of this book. These distinctions are also observed at syntactic, semantic and morphological levels leading to the recognizable deviations from the Standard British English. In this way, American English established its identity as a separate variety. Canadian English is almost a replica of American English due to the geographical proximity as well as strong socio-political nexus between these two countries.

Through this illustration of American English, the nature of deviations in other varieties of English from the Standard British English may largely be understood. Thus, looking from historical perspective, it is fundamentally the British colonialism that spread the tentacles of English in all the colonies. The great industrial revolution of England forced the world gradually to accept its technological superiority that helped England enslave psychologically all the people of the world. This dominance of England generated a strong sense of liking for English among people as there is a common tendency among mankind to learn the language of the dominant or ruling class. This feeling was further reinforced with increasing dependence of global community on the industrial products. These products had English names and many of these names were directly used in other languages due to the lack of instant translation. This popularity of English got a giant fillip with emergence of America as the global leader. The diminishing influence of England in the global arena in the

20th century was substantially compensated for the English language by American supremacy. In this way, the English language continued with its glorious attraction in spite of the transition of global political clout from England to America. Gradually, it turned out to be the language of science and technology contributing most to the uplift of standard of living of mankind in general. All these factors associated with English created such an impression among people about this language that they started treating it as life force in many respects. Today, no society can afford to avoid this language if it wishes to be in the mainstream of global advancement. This attitude of global community towards English is the real cause of emergence of new varieties of English. Its expansion in Arab world where society is predominantly monolingual, that is Arabic-speaking, a new variety of English is almost set to emerge as a large number of people from Arab world will gradually use English evolved under the influence of Arabic as the mother tongue.

10.3 Conclusion

In the light of diversity that is witnessed in the usage of English today at the global level, the concept of conforming or sticking to a particular model like the Standard British English or American English no longer holds water. Though both of these models continue to be used for references, the moot point for a learner of English is to develop global intelligibility that may enable him/her to communicate in English effectively. This objective can be attained only when any learner of English belonging to any corner of the globe aims at casting off the regional influences on his/her English that happen to be the potential source of losing intelligibility. The success of Indian English at global level lends credence to this proposition as English teachers from India are in much demand even in native-English speaking countries.

Exercise

1. What do we mean by a variety of English language? What are the prominent varieties of English?
2. What are the factors responsible for the emergence of varieties of English?
3. How is American English different from the Standard British English?
4. What are the reasons behind popularity of American English?
5. What is the impact of globalization on expansion of English?

Bibliography

Abercrombie, D. *Elements of General Phonetics*, Edinburgh University, 1982.

Anderson, S.R. *The Organisation of Phonology*, Academic Press, 1974.

Armstrong, L.E. *A Handbook of English Intonation*, Heffer, Cambridge, 1949.

Balasubramanian, T. *A Textbook of English Phonetics*, Macmillan India Ltd, 1981.

Ball, Martin J. and Rahilly, Joan. *Phonetics: The Science of Speech*, Arnold, 1999.

Bansal, R.K. *Intelligibility of Indian English*, Ph.D. thesis, University of London, 1966.

Bansal, R.K. and Harrison, J.B. *Spoken English for India*, Orient Longman, 1972.

Bollinger, D.L. (ed). *Intonation, Selected Readings*, Penguin, Harmondswirth, 1972.

Brosnahan, L. and Malmberg, B. *Introduction to Phonetics*, CUP, 1970.

Catford, I.A. *Practical Introduction to Phonetics*, OUP, 1988.

Chomsky and Halle, M. *The Sound Pattern of English*, Harper and Row, New York, 1968.

Clark, J. and Yallop, C. *An Introduction to Phonetics and Phonology*, Blackwell Oxford, 1995.

Collins, B. and Mees. *Practical Phonetics and Phonology*, Routledge, 2013.

Fudge, E.C. (ed). *Intonation, Selected Readings*, Penguin Books, Harmondsworth, 1973.

——. *English Word-Stress*, Allen and Unwin, 1989.

Giegrich, H. *English Phonology*, CUP, 1992.

Gimson, A.C. *An Introduction to the Pronunciation of English*, Edward Arnold, London, 1970.

—— (ed.). *Pronunciation of English*, Hodder, 2008.

Goldsmith, John A. *The Handbook of Phonological Theory*, Blackwell Handbooks in Linguistics, Blackwell Publishers, 1995.

Hocket, Charles F.A. *Manual of Phonology*, Indiana University Publications, 1995.

Jones, D. *The Pronunciation of English*, Cambridge, 1956.

——. *Outline of English Phonetics*, Cambridge, 1956.

——. *An English Pronouncing Dictionary*, London, 1956.

Kingdon, R. *Groundwork of English Intonation*, Longman, London, 1958.

——. *Groundwork of English Stress*, Longman, London, 1958.

Kreedler, Charles. *The Pronunciation of English*, Blackwell, 2004.

Ladefoged, P. *A Course in Phonetics*, Hartcourt Brace Jovanovich, 1982.

Laver, J. *Principles of Phonetics*, CUP, 1994.

Lehiste, L. *Suprasegmentals*, M.I.T. Press, 1970.

Malmberg, B. *Phonetics*, Dover, New York, 1963.

—— (ed.). *Manual of Phonetics*, North Holland, Amsterdam, 1968.

McCully, C. *The Sound Structure of English*, CUP, 2009.

O'Connor, J.D. *Better English Pronunciation*, CUP, 1980.

Pike, K.L. *Phonetics*, Ann Arbor, 1946.

——. *The Intonation of American English*, University of Michigan Press, 1948.

——. *Phonemics: A Technique for Reducing Language to Writing*, Ann Arbor. University of Michigan Press, 1947.

Roach, Peter. *English Phonetics and Phonology: A Practical Course*, CUP, 2009.

Schane, S.A. *Generative Phonology*, Prentice-Hall, New Jersey, 1973.

Sommerstein, A.H. *Modern Phonology*, Arnold, London, 1977.

Swadesh, Morris. "The Phonemic Principle", *Language*, 10 (2), pp. 117-29, 1934.

Tench, P. *The Intonation System of English*, Cassel, London, 1996.

Thomas, C.K. *An Introduction to the Phonetics of American English*, Ronald Press, New York, 1958.

Trager, George L. and Block Bernard. "The Syllabic Phonemes of English", *Language*, 17 (3) pp. 223-46.

Trubetzkoy, N.S. *Principles of Phonology*, (trans.) C.A.M. Baltexe, California University Press, 1969.

Twaddel, W.F. *On Defining the Phoneme*, Baltimore, 1935.

Ward, I.C. *The Phonetics of English*, Heffer, Cambridge, 1948.